a survivor
named trauma

Meyer Aaron Wolpe (author's grandfather) and Anne Wolpe (author's mother) in front of his store on 4½ Street, S.W., Washington, D.C., circa 1913. Unknown street photographer.

a survivor named trauma

Holocaust Memory in Lithuania

Myra Sklarew

Published by State University of New York Press, Albany

© 2020 State University of New York

All rights reserved

No part of this book may be used or reproduced in any manner whatsoever without written permission. No part of this book may be stored in a retrieval system or transmitted in any form or by any means including electronic, electrostatic, magnetic tape, mechanical, photocopying, recording, or otherwise without the prior permission in writing of the publisher.

For information, contact State University of New York Press, Albany, NY
www.sunypress.edu

Library of Congress Cataloging-in-Publication Data

Names: Sklarew, Myra, author.
Title: A survivor named trauma : Holocaust memory in Lithuania / Myra Sklarew.
Description: Albany : State University of New York, 2020. | Includes bibliographical references and index.
Identifiers: LCCN 2019036259 | ISBN 9781438477213 (hardcover : alk. paper) | ISBN 9781438477206 (pbk. : alk. paper) | ISBN 9781438477220 (ebook)
Subjects: LCSH: Holocaust, Jewish (1939–1945)—Lithuania. | Holocaust, Jewish (1939–1945)—Psychological aspects. | Psychic trauma—Lithuania. | Collective memory—Lithuania.
Classification: LCC D804.3 .S594 2020 | DDC 940.53/18094793—dc23
LC record available at https://lccn.loc.gov/2019036259

10 9 8 7 6 5 4 3 2 1

contents

Preface vii

Acknowledgments xiii

Part One

Beginnings 3

Chapter I   In the Ponar Forest 23

Chapter II   Versions 39

Chapter III   Out of Sight 45

Chapter IV   Leiser's Song 55

Chapter V   Lietūkis Garage Massacre ... 83

Part Two

Chapter VI	Return: Witness, Survivor, Next Generation	95
Chapter VII	Trauma Made Manifest: Its Persistent Forms	115
Chapter VIII	Rescue	133
Chapter IX	Who Are Our Teachers?	155
Chapter X	And So I Lived On	175
Notes		187
Bibliography		197
Index		205

preface

A Survivor Named Trauma explores the nature of memory. How do we behave under threat? How do we remember extreme danger? How do subsequent generations deal with their histories—whether as descendants of perpetrators or victims, as those who rescued others or were witnesses to extremity? Or those who separated from their families in early childhood and do not know their origins?

Does it make a difference if the witness is a child or an adult? Or has been previously traumatized and therefore is more vigilant than others? Do we negate the testimony of a survivor if their words are inconsistent with known facts? And what in our own experience here in America turns us toward the events of the Holocaust; what remnants from childhood break open in the present? What do we make of competing versions of history?

A Survivor Named Trauma is told through personal memory via the voices of witnesses and trials after the war, through the experiences of a sewer worker in Lodz, Poland, who rescued a family, and a man from Keidan, Lithuania, who made it his business to document rescuers and murderers after the war.

What is the relationship between those who experienced the Holocaust, with persistent traumatic arousal long after the need for it is present, and our soldiers returning from Iraq or Afghanistan, unable to adapt to life here at home? What is the cost for a child having to hide her identity in order to survive, to vanquish her language, to reconcile the fact that she once had parents and a family?

Why do some people turn to documenting these events and occupation? Why does one man create a museum to preserve the legacy of a people, while his own family was exiled to Siberia for sixteen years? Why do others experience the complete absence of a particular language when we undergo trauma?

Is overwhelming experience processed differently than normal experience? And not only is that experience encoded differently but also differs in its retrieval? Does the greatly increased affective energy at the time of the trauma alter the normal experience of memory?

When two walls collapse, as they are falling they form a bridge. We are now able to bring insights from many disciplines to the study of trauma and memory, and to learn, most importantly, from testimony and reflections of those who have spoken in these pages.

A Survivor Named Trauma is essentially a qualitative study involving interviews with survivors, witnesses, rescuers, and collaborators, as well as descendants and family members, gathered over a twenty-five-year period in Lithuania. This is a country powerfully affected by the Soviet occupation from 1940–41, by the German occupation from 1941–44, and again by the Soviets for forty-five years, ending in 1991.

The work is interdisciplinary, using the tools of neuroscience and neuropsychology, alongside Holocaust studies, Jewish history, and personal memoir. It is an attempt to follow out traumatic experience in a given setting over a period of many years and to learn something about the persistence of trauma and the forms it can take. Given that we live in a time with the largest number of refugees ever recorded in the world, more than 70 million, who have been forced to flee their countries or to hide in place, the subject of trauma and its aftermath takes on especial importance. Our own members of the military, returning from duty, struggle to reconcile their particular traumatic experiences with any sort of a normal life. Current technology has opened the way to verifying specific events and to shed light on experiences not generally known.

A Survivor Named Trauma is divided into two main parts. The opening chapters have to do with points of entry—how this work took hold of my attention and sustained it over a quarter of a century, with multiple versions and perceptions of the same events and the evolution of these perceptions over time. They also address my need to physically engage in the process, to walk the villages and towns of this country, to learn history not only through the texts.

Chapter III deals with the necessity of hiding for the sake of survival, the aftereffects of hiding at the crucial period of identity. A child, suddenly removed from her family, her known language, even her name, is placed into the hands of a rescuer and into a place where she must remain anonymous. Some people must hide in the earth or in a sewer, or crowded together in a barn until the next hiding place can be found. For those who survived, they are left to piece together who they actually are, as well as their parents, their siblings, their rescuers, if possible.

Chapter IV introduces a family member who survived the Kovno Ghetto, Dachau Concentration Camp, forced marches, and the loss of his entire family. Over nine years, in his words, "Leiser's Song" tells this man's perceptions and memories of his experiences, as he circles closer and closer to the center of trauma. In chapter V, "Lietūkis Garage Massacre," various witnesses tell of Jewish men, taken off the street in broad daylight, brought to an automotive garage, and beaten to death. These acts have been witnessed by many, some holding up small children to see. The internalization of memories of this event differs among perpetrators and witnesses, between parent and child who observed this event.

Part Two begins with a circling back, an attempt to locate once more how this twenty-five-year journey began and the curious series of accidental occurrences that were to prove of such significance and become the frame and human map. In chapter VI, I meet the person who was to serve as my guide and friend and, quite by accident, a witness who, by a rare circumstance, lived in the same village as many of my family. Through her assistance, I begin to fill in the details of a survivor relative's experiences. In addition, I learn how a young person views the experience of contemporary Lithuania and is urged by Holocaust survivors to search beneath the surface. She struggles with her expectations of what she would find, which prove to be so dissonant with what she actually witnessed.

Chapter VII deals with persistent forms of trauma, including the erasure of language, the alteration of a familiar landscape, and symbolic condensation, where a single diagonal line can elicit without warning the memory of more than nine thousand inhabitants of the Kovno ghetto being made to walk up a diagonal hill to the Ninth Fort, where they will be killed. Here we look at the neuropsychological view of the formation of trauma and issues of hyperarousal and dissociation, as well as the roles of the amygdala and hippocampus in emotional memory.

Why are some able to take on the role of rescuer in extreme situations? Why does a physician who heads up an orphanage put himself in grave danger by rescuing Jewish children? In chapter VIII, this issue is explored through the experiences not only of one who was rescued by numerous people but also of those who rescued. Who are our best teachers? We look at a man whose own family was deported to Siberia, but who chooses to honor the memory of those in his town by establishing a regional museum "for our lost co-citizens in the Old Market Square near the complex of synagogues." In our interview, he tells why he elected not only commemoration but also to teach about this community's presence for centuries in this town.

Chapter IX continues this exploration through an interview with a major filmmaker who has devoted his cinematic career to documenting Jewish and Roma historical and cultural heritage in Eastern and Central Europe. His film company provides material to educational and documentary film and television programs in Lithuania and abroad. In one of his most striking films, he interviews killers late in their lives, offering a powerful view into the psychology and motivation of killing in the Holocaust.

Regina Kopilevich, fearless guide and archivist, has an uncanny sense of pairing those who have come from all over the world to learn their heritage with information and contacts of enormous meaning. She speaks in our interview about her work. This chapter also features Rachel Kostanian, the founder and former director of the Vilna Gaon Jewish State Museum, the first museum of its kind to deal with the Holocaust in Lithuania. Rūta Puišytė, currently assistant director of the Yiddish Institute at Vilnius University, previously worked at the museum with young volunteers from Austria who served their military time educating students and teachers about the Holocaust. Simonas Davidavičius, executive director of the Sugihara Museum in Kaunas, provides an audiovisual exposition of the former consulate and the work of Chiune Sugihara, who issued visas to some six thousand Jews before leaving Lithuania.

The concluding chapter tells of a survivor who witnessed the mass murder of the Jews of her town: of two thousand, ten survived. She is determined to seek justice. It also includes the stories of survivors who dared to return to Lithuania after a lifetime of absence. It speaks of the specificity of forgetting, of identity, the "fatigue of belonging," and the power and endurance of trauma.

Author's Note: The differences in spelling of names of cities, towns, and villages, as well as proper nouns of persons, organizations, etc., are due to the various languages used, including Yiddish, Hebrew, Polish, Lithuanian, German, and English, as well as the specific endings of words according to gender and marital status in Lithuanian. In this work I have attempted to use spelling appropriate to the speaker and situation.

acknowledgments

One day in 1994 an artist friend arrived at my door bearing an armful of fruits and vegetables, a bouquet of flowers, and a check. Ella Tulin had learned that I was embarking on an overwhelming project. These were her gifts of encouragement. Ella is no longer here in this world for me to thank, but as long as I am around, I offer my gratitude to her for thinking this work possible. To Sarah Blacher Cohen who believed in this project from the beginning. To my sister Betsy Buxer who read through this work early on and provided excellent recommendations and who has been a model for me all my life, and to my sister Janice Eanet who has gone on ahead of us but whose presence and artistry are here among us. To Gordon and Cecelia Knox who invited me to help them establish an artists' community in a fifteenth-century castle in Umbertide, Italy, in 1993. It occurred to me that if I traveled as far as Italy, it might be the perfect time to continue the journey to the home of my mother's people—Lithuania. To fearless Regina Kopilevich whom the fates brought to me for reasons that neither she nor I can recall and without whom very little of my experience in Lithuania would have been possible. In those early days after the collapse of the Soviet Union and the end of a forty-five-year occupation of Lithuania, it was an ideal time to explore the country, but it would have been essentially impossible given the language barriers and necessity to know villages, more than fifteen where my family had once lived. To Anya Martin whose excellent and careful editing of this manuscript has had much to do with the ability to complete this work. To William Frost and the Lucius N. Littauer Foundation for a grant to support this work. Special thanks to Renee Sklarew for her excellent work with the photographs. To Simonas Davidavičius, Dimitri and Shulamit Gelpernas, Abba Kovner and Vitka Kempner, Saulius Beržinis, Yocheved Cartok Inčiūrienė, Rachel Kostanian, Shalom Eilati, Shaul Yannai, Ina Meikšinaitė, Dina Kopilevich, to Michael Kopilevich—my faithful translator, to Ellen Cassedy, Yudel Ronder, Aron and Nijolė Gutman, Vitalija Girčytė, Alexandra Jacovskytė, Adomas Jacovsky, and Leyb Koniuchowsky. A survivor of the Kovno Ghetto, he interviewed more than 150 survivors, located 157 photographs, with detailed accounts from 171 provincial villages. David Leibsohn, scholar/activist/Yiddish soul Dovid Katz, Fruma Kucinskiene, Saulius Sužiedėlis, Eugene Rudder, Moshe Dor, Yehuda and Hana Amichai, David Grossman, Aryeh Shcherbakov, Liudas Truska, Yankel Lopansky, Fania Kentriene, Abe Malnick, Yevsey Zeitlin, Josef Tatsas, Shimon Kaplan, Eta Hecht, Naomi Yodaiken, Sam Schalkowsky, Andrew Cassel, Elena Miknevičienė, Joel Elkes (son of Elchanan Elkes, head of the Ältestenrat in Kovno), Rūta Puišytė, Irena Veisaitė, my cousins Leiser and Ada Wolpe, Stephen Doswald, Emanuel Zingeris, Mark Zingeris, Pauline Zingeris, Victoras Keturakis, son-in-law of Yocheved Inčiurienė, Victoras Keturakis, grandson of Yocheved, Leah Davis, Leonidas Donskis, Charlotte Noshpitz, member of the French Resistance, Joint Distribution Committee Staff, Irwin Arias, NIH, John Schlapobersky, Nancy Goodman and Marilyn Meyers for their support and their own excellent work, Jonas Zurbarkas, Miriam Zaborskienė, David Boder who conducted 130 interviews in nine languages in DP camps, Rimantas Žirgulis,, Ina Navazelskis, Fira Bramson, Michlean Amir and staff at the U.S.H.M.M., Solly Ganor, George Birman, Alexandra Balandienė, Jonas Balandis, Rytas Tamašauskas, Bronius Elijošaitis, Assya Guterman, Riva Lozansky Bogomolnaya, Jacob Bunke, Jonathan Bear, Rasa Greenspon, Irena Guzenberg, and life-friends Jean Nordhaus, Linda Pastan, and Merrill Leffler. To James Peltz, Rafael Chaiken, Ryan Morris, and Kate Seburyamo at SUNY Press. To my Uncle David Wolpe, to Andrew Cassel, to Miriam Beckerman, translator, to Sarah Rebecca Wolpe and Meyer Aaron Wolpe, maternal grandparents, to my mother Anne Wolpe Weisberg, our family historian, and my father Samuel Weisberg, to Bruce and Margaret Meyers, to Renee and Eric Sklarew, to Allison and Danielle Sklarew, to Deborah and Mark Langosch, to Rachel and Daniel Renaud, who enrich my life and have each provided thoughtful and practical help, To my Wolpe family—many whose lives ended in 1941 in Lithuania—and to those who escaped in time that the next generations might live in this world.

∽

Some of the material in this book first appeared as the following: "Trauma Made Manifest: Its Persistent Forms," in *Healing Trauma: The Power of Witnessing*, edited by Evelyn Jaffe Schreiber, 203–19 (New York: International Psychoanalytic Books, 2018); "Leiser's Song," in *The Power of Witnessing: Reflections, Reverberations, and Traces of the Holocaust*, edited by Nancy R. Goodman and Marilyn B. Meyers, 21–44 (New York: Routledge, 2012).

Part One

Beginnings

1

Why seek out the past in a land where so much killing has taken place? By way of answering a question often posed to me regarding my deep attachment to Lithuania, I turn to neuroscience. Our brains contain a map of our bodies. It is not a straightforward map with perfect equivalencies, but a complex cartography. For the eye alone, some thirty regions are required. But if we were to imagine this three-pound umbrella, which presides over our physical parts as a kind of guardian that keeps us intact, we might have at least one of the myriad functions the brain carries out without our having to tell it to.

Once, as director of an artist's community, I found that my body image changed. It was like a large net spread out over hundreds of acres, the land of Yaddo in Saratoga Springs, New York—its buildings, artists, staff, my knowledge of the morning and what I imagined lay ahead of me that day. Before ever stepping from bed, I mentally reviewed furnaces, water sources, septic fields, buildings, keys, foxes, moose and owls, algae in the lakes, gas lines, phone circuits, structural supports. I went over the rooms, their inhabitants, weather conditions, roads plowed for snow emergencies. I reviewed the topography of the landscape. By the time I actually got to my feet and started the daily walk across the grounds, my template was in place, the extension of my body to shelter all of Yaddo.[1] My proprioceptive sense had far more work to do. When I returned to teaching and to my former life, it was strange indeed to diminish that expanded body image.

To recover Lithuania, the home of my family for centuries and generations, I needed to walk the pathways of Lithuania, wherever they might take me, not only through the study of modern history but through the "archives of the feet," as Simon Schama has written. I shall always be grateful that it has been possible to do so in my lifetime, that the freedom from domination under the Soviets that came to Lithuania in 1990–91 enabled people like me to wander without restriction through the lands of our people, to come to know something about them and to complete the map of the body, to reintegrate the body through a renewed understanding of the physical and mental landscapes where our forebears lived and died.

I am reminded of a legend about a great Kabbalist, told to me in 1970 in Safed, Israel. When he was buried, he was unable to rest. He called and called for his son. And until he was buried next to his son, he could not achieve eternal rest.

As Michael Steinlauf writes in "Beyond the Evil Empire: Freedom to Remember or Freedom to Forget?":

> First and foremost, there is the powerful, pervasive sense of place. Cities, towns, streets, marketplaces, courtyards, mezuzahs still outlined over doorways; synagogues and cemeteries . . . the Vistula River, cutting through the Polish heartland, whose water, the writer Sholem Asch once declared, spoke to him in Yiddish; these and countless other sites saturated with the visible and invisible traces of Jewish presence, are all still there, a Jewish geography as yet unmapped, but as real as any. Side-by-side, sometimes in the same places, are the death sites: remnants of camps, graves, crematoria. Can we deal with this? Can we finally accept the challenge of seeing everything, the life as well as the death?[2]

2

Lithuania is a country only slightly larger than West Virginia, its population approximately 2.5 million in 1940. Imagine, then, Lithuania's position during the Soviet occupation (population 191.7 million) from

1940–41. And from 1941-July 1944 under German occupation (population 87.1 million).

It is a country that has been occupied multiple times—from the ninth to eleventh centuries by the Vikings, with raids between Lithuania and Poland in the twelfth century, military confrontations with German settlers, with a series of wars between the Polish-Lithuanian Commonwealth and Sweden, with the occupation by the Soviets from 1940–41, by the Germans from 1941–44, and from July 1944 until 1990–91 by the Soviets. That Lithuania has managed to hold onto a common language and any sort of a common heritage is remarkable.

And if what I have been told by those who lived through the German occupation is true, when the Germans arrived in Lithuania in 1941, many thought by the strength of their forces that this was to be a permanent occupation. Therefore, when a person or a family or a community decided to rescue a person, they assumed that it was for an indefinite period of time. It was not a brief commitment. And the retribution for doing so might result in the murder of the rescuer, of the entire family of the rescuer, of the whole community.

Some have written about the alternative. If the Lithuanians had risen up against the Germans and even if they had succeeded, which is totally improbable, would they have fared better than under the Soviets? Of course, they had no knowledge that they would eventually end up exactly in that way, not for a year or two but for forty-five years under the Soviets. There *are* examples of whole communities refusing to kill but they are rare. Le Chambon in France is one, where each member of the community hid and rescued Jews.[3] The townspeople of Le Chambon were an anomaly in France as descendants of the Huguenots who had been persecuted since the sixteenth century. Each person had fought his own battle against those who would crush him. Their rebellion was whole. It was not a matter of a leader establishing the position of resistance for the rest, but a position that rested squarely within each inhabitant of the town. One example of the reliability of the individual consciousness may be seen in the transformation of Bible study leaders. There were thirteen groups led by youngsters for the purpose of study. When the Germans occupied France, these groups became the communications network and their leaders the moving spirits of the rescue operation. Pastor Trocme gave most of his instruction (Bible and resistance!) to these leaders. He saw to it that he was the only person in Le Chambon who knew of the entire operation, that the groups operated independently of one another, so that if one leader was caught and tortured, he would not reveal enough to destroy the whole rescue machine. Each leader had to make swift, intelligent decisions on his own when Trocme was not available.

When Pastor Trocme, in the French Army in 1921, was sent on a mapping mission in Morocco, he was issued a gun and cartridges. As a believer in nonviolence, he left his equipment at the depository. Asked to explain, his lieutenant pointed out that he had endangered the lives of the entire group by his action and that he should have made such a decision earlier. This lesson was invaluable. Thus, the forms of resistance in Le Chambon began early with small refusals: no ringing of the church bells for Marshal Philippe Petain, the head of the Vichy state, no Fascist salute. This was the form of the "kitchen struggle" in Le Chambon. When the Vichy police came to take Pastor Trocme to prison, the people of Le Chambon came with gifts: candles, biscuits, toilet paper upon which verses of consolation from the Bible had been written to remind him that he was still human. Magda Trocme, the pastor's wife, when confronted by the first Jew asking for help, simply opened the door and said "Come in." I had occasion to meet her and her daughter Nelly when they came to this country more than thirty years ago. She spoke of those war years. The plainspoken woman before me made no claim for what she had done. And though the war ended, her work never did. The Trocmes became a model and an encouragement for the conscientious objectors in this country during World War II, according to our former U.S. Poet Laureate, William Stafford, who worked in C.O. camps during the war because of his decision not to serve in the military. "When did you decide to go another way?" I asked him once. It was a hard decision in the face of a patriotic war. "I didn't," he responded. "The world went a different way."

These important lessons—that one must be prepared to be human, and that timing is crucial—remind me of what I have heard said by concentration camp survivors: one must be wary of the first, smallest injustice. Through the entryway of the first injustice does the next come.

The decision to act in the face of injustice does not come when a man is being shoved into a ravine with a bullet in his neck.

3

How do we behave under dire threat? How do we remember extreme danger and its recurring trauma as if it were happening in the present? Hopefully, what Lithuania has to teach us can be applied to the future and future behavior under duress. How does the individual response differ from the group response? How do subsequent generations deal with their histories—whether as descendants of the killers or the killed, of those who witnessed what happened, of those who rescued others, and of those who do not know their origins.

Two powerful examples include the request of a young man from Austria who decided that he wanted to serve his required military time in community service—an option made available in Austria through the *Gedenkdienst*, Austrian Holocaust Memorial Service begun in 1992. He requested a fourteen-month service in the Vilna Gaon Jewish Memorial Museum in Vilnius, Lithuania, in 1996. Though there was some initial resistance and uncertainty by employees of the museum, he was invited to do so. When I asked him why he decided to come to Lithuania, he said that he discovered later that his grandfather and his uncle had served in the Wehrmacht in Lithuania during the war and were involved in the killing of the Jews—something he had not known initially. Thus began a series of remarkable volunteers from Austria, every fourteen months or so, who were invaluable in sharing what they were learning with teachers and students about their former Jewish neighbors, and about events they had not known of, in editing and writing documents, in preparing museum exhibitions, in presenting symposia on the Holocaust, and in learning about a country known only vaguely to them. In one case that I know of, this activity was costly to the young volunteer in terms of the severance of family relations. In September 2006, this activity culminated in a symposium, "Commemoration of Holocaust Victims: 10 Years of Gedenkdienst Activity in Lithuania." This work of education and understanding continues to this day. I was able to get to know these young people during my times there, helping to edit documents for the museum.

I accompanied one of these volunteers to religious services on the Jewish New Year. He had never before entered a synagogue. It was cold that day and a cold rain made the walk there unpleasant. After the service, as we walked down the stairs toward the street, a double rainbow illuminated the entire sky.

A second example occurred during Holocaust Remembrance Day in Lithuania on September 23, 2011. I was standing in the town square in Kaunas among a group of a hundred people. Various people took turns speaking. One was a Holocaust survivor who had been hidden as a child, one of the few who survived. After the event, some of the younger people, who had never before heard a survivor tell her experiences, gathered around her to ask questions and to continue the conversation. Among official speakers, a young man stood up and walked to the microphone. His words: "My grandfather and my grandfather's brother have done terrible things during the War and they have placed a burden on my whole life. I ask forgiveness." The priests comforted this young man after he spoke. His grandfather was a man who, when the killing was too much for the other killers, would take their places. He was part of a killing unit that traveled from village to village. And I knew that his grandson speaking publicly would bring shame to his family. Standing there that day, we understood how difficult it was for this young man to speak.[4]

4

I have started this book many times. Perhaps it wants to be brought into existence as a series of beginnings . . . no middle, no end. As in Italo Calvino's *If on a winter's night a traveler*—a book built of multiple openings. Yet its contents are too serious to concern the reader with its difficult birth. Still, the writer wonders why the writing is so difficult. Can it be more so than standing in the killing fields? Or walking the periphery of a tumuli filled with the murdered who were once members of her family? Is it in that ditch that I now walk among these pages, trying not to let my words desecrate their graves, keeping my balance?

And will it seem strange to some that we are a people who often do not know the precise birthplace of our grandfathers? As for a grandmother—records were scarce. Military records. Yes. Revision lists. Yes. With the man's name. Box tax records. Candle tax records. For that reason—that I may never know precisely where my grandmother was born, apart from the province, Kovno (Kaunas) Gubernia—I will leave on my gravestone the name of my maternal antecedents along with my father's name.

This is a book about memory. "I think that if I recall something," Borges's father once told him, "for example, if today I look back on this morning, then I get an image of what I saw this morning. But if tonight, I'm thinking back on this morning, then what I'm really recalling is not the first image, but the first image in memory. So that every time I recall something, I'm not recalling it really, I'm recalling the last time I recalled it, I'm recalling my last memory of it. So that really, I have no memories whatever. I have no images whatever, about my childhood, about my youth." Borges notes that "if in every repetition you get a slight distortion, then in the end you will be a long way off from the issue."[5]

This is a book about forgetting. And about the ways in which memory is constructed. And it is a book about trauma, the ways we devise to bring harm to one another. It is about the different kinds of responses to trauma.

"The highest form of revenge," according to Borges, "is oblivion."[6] So perhaps instead of a book, what took place here should be relegated to silence, to oblivion. Better to let it be a gathering place for what is remembered. May the voices of many come to inhabit these pages.

5

In the history of nations, the stories have sometimes been buried. As in Pompeii, its citizens caught in the ash and fire rain of an erupting volcano. In the midst of their afternoon. We see them at the moment of their transformation. From living souls to frozen immobility. Even the household creatures. What they knew, they have taken with them. What we know of them, we have taken from parchment, from conjecture, from scientific reconstruction.

In Lithuania, even years later, it still seems too dangerous for full openness. Thus, we read that three thousand documents—Soviet Lithuanian secret documents from the late fifties and early sixties—have "accidentally" been recycled for use as toilet paper, documents that clearly could incriminate some still alive.

We speak of those who attempted to hide their bodies that they would not be murdered. And we speak of those who even now must still hide from the truth of those years. For here is a country occupied more often than not in its long history, by virtue of its placement in the world between powerful nations, often at war with one another, who thought nothing of scooping up Lithuania, binding her first to one territory, then another.

The hope is that the avenues of exploration and the work that has resulted might be of use to others as they do research in this field. It may be possible, by hearing out—as carefully as we know how—the stories we are told by those who lived these years, to come to the faint outlines, to the threshold of understanding of what may, in fact, never be understood.

6

Who is qualified to tell this? As a participant in a Holocaust conference some years ago with presentations largely by historians, I was surprised to learn that Holocaust testimony was viewed by many as "unreliable." Its subjective nature often contained historical inaccuracies, according to some. I had been interviewing survivors, witnesses, rescuers, and some collaborators in Lithuania for many years and had become aware of the importance of the inconsistences in testimony. In the case of one particularly horrendous massacre that initiated the freedom to commit others, I gathered testimony from twenty witnesses. Some had been children at the time, others adults. We had everything to learn from the great variety of testimony, the entire panorama of human response, the inexact nature and selectivity of memory.

Dominick LaCapra, in *Writing History, Writing Trauma*, speaks of testimonies as supplying not only documentary evidence but also an understanding of "experience and its aftermath, including the role of memory and its lapses." LaCapra cites the experience of Dori Laub, psychoanalyst and interviewer for the Yale Fortunoff collection of survivor videos and himself a survivor. Laub tells of a woman who in Auschwitz recalls "four chimneys going up in flames, exploding," as an uprising takes place. Colleagues at a conference later determined that the fact that only a single chimney exploded rendered the woman's memory fallible and therefore they could not rely on her entire account of events. Laub comments that the number of chimneys blown up was not of importance but that the woman actually "testified to an event that broke the all compelling frame of Auschwitz, where Jewish armed revolts just did not happen. . . . That was historical truth."[7]

Perhaps some fixed truth is there to be found. Perhaps, unlike our knowledge in physics where our very presence observing a phenomenon alters what we see, there is some truth to be captured. But what is it we have when we gather twenty or fifty or a hundred accounts of a single episode—9/11 or the recent tornados or the crash scene of an airplane or a holdup—and find as many versions of the events as there are people observing.

What can we learn from these disparate accounts? Does it matter if the witness is a child or an adult? Related to those who are in harm's way? Previously traumatized and therefore more vigilant than others? Trained to observe or taken unawares?

Many years ago I was called to testify in a medical malpractice case where a patient who had gone in to the hospital for elective surgery had suddenly stopped breathing and ended up in a vegetative state. The lawyer called upon the surgical technicians, anesthesiologist, nurses, surgeons to testify. Had the anesthesiologist failed to turn on the apparatus that measured breathing levels or heart rate; had he ignored the signals when they showed up? At that time no surgical checklist was in place. Had any of the others in the operating theatre neglected their roles in this procedure? As the trial proceeded, day after day, as each made his case to prove his innocence, it became clear that for whatever reason, we would not learn what the failing had been. Had the patient, with an existing malformation that made intubation difficult, been the unwitting culprit in this drama?

Would we invalidate the Kovno (Kaunas) Ghetto police records kept daily because they do not contain the larger knowledge of events and circumstances that were more fully available to Dr. Elchanan Elkes and other leaders of the Kovno Ältestenrat? Does this diminish their authority and enormous value?

Or banish the writings *in extremis* of the Hungarian poet Miklos Radnoti whose small notebook was found in his trousers pocket when the mass grave was exhumed in 1946 containing a poem he wrote as his violinist friend was shot in the head and as Radnoti was about to die: "You'll be finished off like this—/I muttered to myself—so just lie still."[8] Will we ever decipher the meaning of a man who opens his eyes to what is to befall him and is able to write in that critical moment, to record for others? Or would we dismiss Dan Pagis: "I am learning/the declensions and ascensions of/silence."[9] As Robert Alter writes: "[T]his use of distanced and multiple voices is linked with an impulse to pull apart the basic categories of existence and reassemble them in strange configurations that expose the full depth of the outrage perpetrated."[10] Pagis, drawing on the *Yigdal*, writes: "And he in his mercy left nothing of me that would die./And I fled to him, floated up weightless, blue,/ forgiving—I would even say: apologizing—/smoke to omnipotent smoke/ that has no face or image."[11] And the miraculous transformation that such a survivor could become the expositor of the "luminous horizon of medieval Hebrew poetry,"[12] We have only begun to learn what Pagis had to teach us.

Or Avrom Sutzkever, who could create poems while hiding in a coffin or struggling to stay alive in a lime pit where he sees his own blood run into the lime like lines of poetry. Who refused the victim's role, transforming his life into art. Or Ephraim Sten, who could address the child he had been, hiding in a hole in the earth, and cross the chasm back to his earlier days with the full weight of adult life. Others chose to radically alter their language, or abandon it altogether. Amir Gilboa calls upon the biblical Isaac, only this time no angel comes to his rescue. Nelly Sachs uses liturgy to express the loss. Paul Celan once said: "Only one thing remained reachable, close and secure amid all losses: language."[13] Celan, who cauterized German, who implanted human feeling into the "time-crevasse," into the "honeycomb-ice." Kadya Molodovsky pleads with God to choose another people. S. Y. Agnon forecast the degeneration of Jewish culture in Eastern Europe. Yehuda Amichai once told me that after two uncles had washed the bodies of two relatives who had been beaten to death, the entire extended family from Wurzburg, Germany, packed up and left for Palestine. How was it that some could read the signs of danger and take action, even this family deeply embedded in the religious culture of its place and time?

We have heard for years—"No poetry after Auschwitz." Or to put it more accurately, *"Nach Auschwitz ein Gedicht zu schreiben ist barbarisch"* (After Auschwitz, to write a poem is barbaric). What did Theodor Adorno, writing in 1949 and so often quoted, mean by this? And how did this become such an essential criticism of Holocaust representation?

Michael Rothberg[14] speaks of Samuel Beckett and Franz Kafka's internalization of the disaster and its sustaining of an absent "presence," where "art's barbarity is not refuted but enacted in order to present the barbarity of the age." Sixteen years later, Adorno wrote in "The Liquidation of the Self" that his words had given "rise to a discussion [he] did not anticipate . . ." He intended "to point to the hollowness of the resurrected culture of that time—it could equally well be said, on the other hand, that one must write poems." Adorno objected not to the representation of the Holocaust in art but to the transfiguration of the Holocaust as it is made into art which removes some of the horror. He objects to the redemptive function of art, the notion that the Holocaust could yield something positive. Adorno's writings suggest the need for new forms of representation capable of registering the traumatic shock of modern genocide, to translate knowledge of extremity to a mass audience. Adorno brought together the questions of Holocaust representation and education at a moment when they had not yet been fully articulated. Others have talked about the untranslatable trauma of the Holocaust whose only language is silence.[15]

Jean Amery has written: "To be a Jew, that meant for me, from this moment on, to be a dead man on leave. . . . Our sole right, our sole duty was to disappear from the face of the earth. Whoever has succumbed to torture can no longer feel at home in the world. Trust in the world, which already collapsed . . . at the first blow, but in the end, under torture, fully, will not be regained. That one's fellow man was experienced as the anti-man remains in the tortured person as accumulated horror. It blocks the view into a world in which the principle of hope rules."[16]

Peter Kenez, a Hungarian survivor, writes in his memoir when asked what he was afraid of: "People."[17] Elie Wiesel, in a figure in *The Gates of the Forest*, writes: "My name left me. You might say that it's dead. It went away one day, without reason, without excuse, it forgot to take me along. That's why I have no name. Of course, I looked for it, but without success."[18] In a few words he has encompassed the issue of loss of identity. We will return to this subject later. Who are we when we must give up our language, religion, parentage, culture, landscape, even our sense of wholeness of body, in order to survive? And does it matter if we are four years old or fifty?

Whatever we decide about how the Holocaust is to be transmitted and how survivors were able to take up their lives once more, I know of one person who was able to live afterward through art. Leiser Wolpe, who survived the Kovno Ghetto, the murder of his father, the burning alive of his brother, the death of his mother in a concentration camp, and of all whom he held dear, who survived Dachau and forced marches and tuberculosis, believes that he could not have lived afterward had he not married an artist, a painter, who painted him in the garden and whose work stood as a veil between him and the darkness from which he emerged.[19] But even this did not erase from him the image of a sea of blood, which he saw the first time he entered a body of water after the war ended.

7

History and Memory: Once history was permanent as a mountain. Until I read in my father's book the tale Pliny the Younger reported to Tacitus about his uncle's death and the sudden appearance of a peculiar cloud:

> I cannot give you a more exact description of its figure, than by resembling it to that of a pine-tree, for it shot up a great height in the form of a trunk, which extended itself at the top into a fort of branches . . . it appeared sometimes bright and sometimes dark and spotted, as it was either more or less impregnated with earth and cinders.[20]

This was Mt. Vesuvius erupting. Prelude to the annals of a town abruptly closed: Pompeii. So much for the permanence of mountains. And soon enough thereafter, skepticism rendered textbook history open to debate.

8

Perhaps the earliest doubt occurred in 1941: I was just seven. I had come home from school one day to find my mother and father sitting on the stairs halfway between the first and second floors of our house. What terrible news had brought my father home from work? We had, for weeks, been practicing air-raid drills in school, hiding under our desks or in hallways to avoid the bombs that could fall at any moment. Or the amphibious tanks (I wasn't sure what that word meant) that could come crashing through the classroom window. Our precautions, in retrospect, were flimsy.

Though I could not embrace the full meaning of the Holocaust, from that day forward I knew that something quite terrible was happening to Jewish people. And not only to a people in the abstract, but to those in our family who still lived in Europe.

In fact, by then—though we did not know it yet—two-thirds of the Jews of Lithuania, home to my mother's people for centuries, had been murdered. In villages throughout Lithuania, massacres had taken place beginning in late June 1941. Under the Molotov-Ribbentrop Pact, the Soviet-Nazi treaty of 1939, Eastern Europe was partitioned. The Baltic states came under the jurisdiction of the Soviets. The Soviet occupation began on June 15, 1940. A year later, June 22, 1941, Nazi Germany attacked the Soviet Union. "Operation Barbarossa" opened its assault on

Lithuania. The Red Army fled. With the arrival of German occupation forces, the entire Jewish populations of more than 200 villages and towns were massacred.

Family letters only now recovered and translated, coded to pass through the censors, indicate the imminent danger:

> Kaunas, December 28, 1940
>
> You mentioned in your letter *Gan Eden* [Garden of Eden], but you forgot that there is also such a place called *Gehinom* [Hell] . . . we beg of you to do everything in your power to make it possible for us to meet with you.
>
> Your brother, Jacob

From Kovno Ghetto to Dachau Concentration Camp to his death. His wife to die in Stutthof Concentration Camp. His son, death at Dachau. One daughter drowned moments before reaching shore after being thrown from a ship in the Baltic Sea in a desperate attempt by the Nazis to erase their crimes. A second daughter, a cousin, survived the years in the ghetto, forced labor, a concentration camp, forced marches, washed up on the shore at Kiel, Germany, and was rescued by a British soldier who thinking her dead kicked her. "This one moves," he said.

This recollection of my cousin reminded me of Miklos Radnoti, mentioned earlier, a Hungarian Jew who wrote—days before his own death on a forced march—of lying next to his violinist friend after a mass shooting, believing his turn would be next: "I fell beside him; his body turned over,/already as taut as a string about to snap./Shot in the back of the neck. That's how you too will end,/I whispered to myself; just lie quietly./Patience now flowers into death./*Der springt noch auf,* a voice said above me."[21] Signs of life brought rescue for my cousin; another bullet for the violinist.

9

Where shall we go for the truth? Where does it reside? In the hands of the murderers? In the records of the Nazis, the Einsatzgruppen reports?

In German photographs showing mothers holding up their small children to witness the clubbing to death of Jewish men in the Lietukis Garage massacre? In the recollections of those very children? In the testimony of survivors? Witnesses? Rescuers? Historians? In the earth itself, uncovered by forensic scientists? In fact, in recent days a team of archaeologists, using ground-penetrating radar and a form of tomography, have located a 115-foot tunnel created by the hands and spoons of Jews whose job it was to dig up and burn the remains of some one hundred thousand (Jews, Poles, and Russians) who had been killed in pits in the Ponar (Paneriai) Forest in 1944 outside of Vilnius. Of the eighty who started the work, some eleven survived to provide witness to what was done at Paneriai (Holocaust Escape Tunnel, NOVA, April 2017).

Shlomo Breznitz has written in his memoir *Memory Fields*: "There are many different truths, all quite plausible, and often very tempting. And then there is time, with tricks of its own. The fields of memory are like a rich archeological site, with layer upon layer of artifacts from different periods."[22]

Is what was told in 1946 more valid than what is remembered in 1990? Are the Displaced Persons reports gathered just after the war more reliable? Why are historians disturbed by the reactions of Holocaust survivors when survivors take issue with their findings? What about the mainstream party line? Is the idea that the number of killers was equal to the number of rescuers valid? And if so, what bearing does it have on our understanding of the Holocaust? How are villagers influenced by the various rationales offered to counter guilt and blame? What does it mean that a man leaned out of an apartment window in Vilnius, Lithuania, in 1996 during a walk by Holocaust survivors in the former Vilna Ghetto and shouted: "I thought we had got rid of you all. What are you looking at? We should have killed all of you." What does it mean that a rescuer, who risked his own life, his family, his neighbors, comes to talk with me and the woman he rescued and brings along his young grandson to translate? Why does he want his grandson to be so deeply involved in the transmission of this information? A man who makes nothing of what he did. Clearly, the child has already learned what so many adults will never be able to.

"Fate brought me together in those terrible days with very good people, some Lithuanians and some Poles," writes Yocheved Inčiūrienė, a survivor. "I have to stress the special role Jonas Saunoris played in my life: without any conditions he agreed to take a completely unknown and strange girl and hide her, not being afraid of any dangers . . . he accepted me like a member of his family and guarded me like a true sister. . . . It is a pity that such dedicated people were significantly fewer than was required to help the condemned Jews."[23]

10

"When the past is seriously contended among different groups of stakeholders in a society or when the past has the potential of assigning guilt to large groups of people," write professors G. E. Schafft and William H. Kincade of American University, "public history becomes contentious."[24]

> Its stigma may be dispelled through: (1) outright denial—ignoring the events by glossing over them or replacing them with other public deeds; (2) comparisons with similar horrors that thereby render them relatively harmless; (3) creating boundaries through a distancing from the events in time, place, or persons; or (4) even wearing the stigma as a badge of honor. . . . How public figures . . . interpret these symbolic representations of history is also important to the civic persona of a community.[25]

We find competing versions of history in Lithuania. The generational differences alone are significant. A rare school teacher shortly after the end of the Soviet occupation, willing to broach the subject of the Holocaust, to help open a dialogue between grandchildren and grandparents, has risked censure by the community. For years, Jews were seen as creators of their own downfall for alleged participation in the NKVD, for alleged responsibility in the exile to Siberia of Lithuanians—though more Jews proportionately were deported to Siberia than Lithuanian non-Jews—and for their embrace of the Russian occupation. As we know, a tenet of Nazism was to make the Jews complicit in their own suffering and death: the Sonderkommando forced to lead Jews to the gas chambers, the kapos put in charge of other prisoners in the concentration camps, those shot in mass graves forced to dig the pits beforehand, a man condemned to hang forced to hang another first, the use of the Judenrat, the Jewish councils in the ghettos, by the Nazis.

Today, organizations and individuals both within Lithuania and beyond her shores are making numerous efforts to bring light into the discussion of the past. The Holocaust is part of the educational curriculum.

11

And what of memory itself? Primo Levi writes, in *The Drowned and the Saved*:

> Human memory is a marvelous but fallacious instrument. . . . The memories which lie within us are not carved in stone; not only do they tend to become erased as the years go by, but often they change, or even grow, by incorporating extraneous features.[26]

Charlotte Delbo, in *La memoire et les jours*, speaks of past events not relegated to the distance but always next to her: "Auschwitz is there, unalterable, precise . . . enveloped in the skin of memory, an impermeable skin that isolates it from my present self. Unlike the snake's skin, the skin of memory does not renew itself. Oh, it may harden further. . . . Alas, I often fear lest it grow thin, crack, and the camp get hold of me again. . . . I live within a twofold being."[27] When the skin of memory fails to hold, she becomes the person she was in the death camp—frozen, hungry, filthy, exhausted. In dreams, the act of will cannot hold, the life alongside her life breaks through. Yet in the dream she cries out and the sound of her cry wakes her. She emerges from Auschwitz once again. And gives voice to her experience *in extremis*.

12

And what is the nature of the survivor's loss? Jean Amery, tortured by the SS, speaks of the loss of "trust in the world" in *At the Mind's Limits*: "A slight pressure by the tool-wielding hand is enough to turn the other—

along with his head, in which are perhaps stored Kant and Hegel, and all nine symphonies, and the World as Will and Representation—into a shrilly squealing piglet at slaughter."[28] One cannot be at home here. "That one's fellow man was experienced as the anti-man remains in the tortured person as accumulated horror. It blocks the view into a world in which the principle of hope rules."

13

In *The Story of a Life,* Aharon Appelfeld, who witnessed the shooting of his mother when he was eight, managed to escape from a labor camp and wandered alone for several years in Ukrainian forests in constant danger. About his memory of those years, he writes:

> Everything that happened is imprinted within my body and not within my memory. The cells of my body apparently remember more than my mind, which is supposed to remember. For years after the war, I would walk neither in the middle of the sidewalk nor in the middle of the road. I always clung to the walls, always staying in the shade, and always walking rapidly, as if I were slipping away. As a rule I'm not given to crying, but even the most casual partings can reduce me to tears.[29]

Every source that can teach us is valuable. From every discipline and every angle, we need to look at what happened, to draw away the *cordon sanitaire* around memory that Primo Levi speaks of and examine all that comes into our view.

And if we could make our way through all that has been written, recorded, filmed, photographed, testified to, if we had time and life enough and the capacity to encompass the record of what has taken place, which of the myriad records would begin to tell us how we might understand this bestial epoch?

In the words of a survivor, "There is a world of difference . . . between the professionals engaged in theoretical, philosophical approaches and the real thing." He goes on to say that no one can imagine the "inferno, the tragical need to bend coldly and ruthlessly values, to abandon family values and tradition, to think cold, hard and as a Darwinian." And he challenges any PhD, historian or researcher who was not directly involved in the Holocaust "to let us Survivors speak. We are a vanishing species. Our impressions are subjective but irreplaceable. I do not consider them as the Bible, and history will consist of our testimony balanced with viewpoints of historians. The task is not easy."

As for writing the Holocaust, perhaps Paul Celan understood it best—"*auch ohne/Sprache*"—even without language must it be written. It must be kept, imprinted in the language of memory. But memory itself is not the guardian who will keep us from devising the harm we bring to one another.

Chapter I

IN THE PONAR FOREST

1

I am at the bottom of an excavated pit in the forest called Ponar (Paneriai). I kneel on the sandy ground and dig my fingers into the earth. Just as when I bury someone I love, I take a handful of soil to place on the coffin. Only this time I find in my palm a round nub of bone. For here is where they were brought, here shot in the back of the head, here fallen or thrown into this pit. And here, later, dug up and burned.

    I knelt there, registering the shape and weight of the bone, which my hand can still feel, years later. The body's memory, some would say. Suddenly I become aware that I am not alone. High above me, standing on the rim of the pit, a small family group stares down at me as if they have seen a ghost. I am startled by their presences and rise to my feet, still holding the bony remnant of all that transpired there. I climb out of the pit, but they are frozen at the top. *Laba Diena,* I call to them. But my words ricochet off the trees like jagged stones. And no word comes back to me from those assembled there. I start to walk out of the forest. I look back several times. But they do not move from the spot.

    Were they Dante and his faithful guide Virgil, standing on that rim, witnessing the plight of those condemned below, remembering? Or are they simply out for a walk? I have seen villagers plucking mushrooms from the base of trees. I have seen women with small enamel jugs, like

Ponar—excavated massacre pit

Ponar Memorial pit

Ponar ladder used for burning bodies

the one my Lithuanian grandmother used, collecting wild strawberries from the earth of this place. How long does blood take to become salt and water? How long before bone is nothing more than particles of calcium, no trace of anything human here? Are the berries flavored by their human contribution? Do the mushrooms' earthy scent bear signals of something once alive? The mycelium, four hundred years in the making, nourished by countless wars, by betrayals, by blood and bone, by the tears of the dead, by hair and skin. Every hill is suspect, every ravine, every tree. If you put your foot down on the earth in Keidan (Kėdainiai) or Dotnuva or Ponar, if you stop walking and read the shape of the earth under your foot, is it a remnant of someone you knew, someone you almost remembered. In Kovno a man keeps the bones of his family from Ponar in a glass jar on his bookshelf, bones and a bit of earth. A man keeps a list of the killers. Sometimes he sends them anonymous letters, warning them. Sometimes he confronts them directly. He has nothing more to lose. A man keeps a list of the righteous. He documents acts of kindness and rescue, the names of those who risked their own lives to save others.

I am not at home in prayer. Though I wish I could bring myself to recite the Kaddish here, the prayer for the dead. To ritualize this visit. But perhaps it is enough to come here each year. That it not be entirely forgotten. As it will be, one day. It is as if a life fills up with all of the world that will fit within it, and then suddenly that life is gone. Sometimes it takes years. Sometimes, as at Ponar, the lives were only partly filled; sometimes barely anything of the world had time to pour its language into the life. Infants. Small children. Only recently awakened into their lives.

Why have they dug up this pit? When all the others are closed and covered over with green grass and quiet as if the secrets of what happened here are buried deep in the earth. Are they looking for artifacts? This is a historian's word. An anthropologist's. An archaeologist's. Whatever small thing came loose from them as they went into the air, as they fell to earth. My words have no validity. Historians will tell you that. Only the pieced-together musings of one who wasn't there. And she could return a hundred times and not a single tree would speak to her. Not one to tell her what it witnessed. How many rains have come to wash away the blood that covered trunk and bark and leaf. How many winters to bury them over again. And how many births in spring to obliterate the death that abides here.

2

Kazimierz Sakowicz moved to a frame cottage in Ponar in 1939. The house, in a wooded area adjacent to a fuel storage facility created during the Soviet occupation (1940–41) for the nearby airbase, provided an excellent vantage point to witness what took place here. Though the project was never completed, a series of pits twelve to thirty-two meters in diameter and five to eight meters deep had been excavated for fuel tanks. These became the sites for the execution of some seventy thousand Jews, twenty thousand Poles, and eight thousand Russians. Sakowicz, a journalist, secretly observed and recorded in his diary the daily killings at Ponar beginning July 11, 1941. "The Shaulists do the shootings, striplings of seventeen to twenty-five years. The Šaulių Sąjunga (Rifleman's Association) had been a paramilitary nationalist organization before Lithuania fell into Soviet hands."[1]

In addition to his direct observations, Sakowicz "made inquiries among his neighbors and talked with railroad employees, farmers who bought the victims' clothes, and the Lithuanian killers, or 'Ponary riflemen' themselves," according to Rachel Margolis, the only member of her family to survive the Holocaust. Held in the Vilna (Vilnius) Ghetto, Margolis escaped and joined the partisans and after the war began to locate and decipher fragments of Sakowicz's diary. The diary was not published until 1999 in Polish and not until 2005 in English which, according to Margolis, was likely so because of its evidence of the extent of Lithuanian collaboration in the deaths of so many. Though survivors have written testimony and memoirs, this diary is rare in that it offers direct testimony from a bystander.

3

Q: Attorney General: You learned that in Ponar they were simply murdering Jews?

A: Witness Kovner: If you will allow me, I shall describe the thing which is engraved in my memory most of all.

Q: What was engraved in your memory most of all?

A: This is the story of a woman named Sara Menkes, who was rescued from the pit, and she told me of the execution of a group of women, in October 1941. She told me about this several weeks later. In this group there was, amongst others, one who you could say was a pupil of mine. For several months I had taught her in the gymnasium in Vilna. Her name was Tsherna Morgenstern. I shall describe it briefly: they were taken to Ponar. After they had waited at some point, a group of them was taken and lined up in a row. They were told to undress. They undressed down to their shirts. A line

Abba Kovner in Vilna

of men of the Einsatzgruppen stood facing them. An officer came out in front of them, looked at the row of women, and his glance fell on this Tsherna Morgenstern. She had wonderful eyes, a tall, upstanding girl with long plaits. He looked at her for a long time, smiled and said: "Take one step forward." She was terrified, as all of them were. At that moment nobody spoke, nobody asked anything. She remained where she was, evidently panic stricken, and did not step forward. He ordered her, asking: "Hey—don't you want to live—you are so beautiful—I say to you: 'Take one step forward.'" He said to her: "It would be a pity to bury such beauty in the ground. Walk, but don't look backwards. There is a path here, you know this path, walk along it." For a moment she hesitated and then she began walking. The rest of us—Sara Menkes told me—gazed at her with a look in our eyes. I don't know whether it was only of fear and also of envy. She walked forward weakly. And then he, the officer, drew his revolver and shot her, as the first, in her back.

4

Poet and translator Shirley Kaufman wrote in her introduction to Abba Kovner's book *A Canopy in the Desert: Selected Poems*:[2] "[A] young girl crawled up over the thousands of bodies in the pits of Ponar and made her way . . . through a frozen forest back to the Vilna Ghetto. No one could believe her story, forty thousand Jews dead in a ditch. But Abba Kovner listened and believed. He was twenty-two years old. He wrote the first Jewish call to arms in the Vilna Ghetto, a pathetic call since there was no way to get guns or ammunition."

Two years later, with "nothing ahead but death and madness," Abba Kovner became the leader of their fighting resistance, the United Partisan Organization. They began to take people out of the ghetto through the sewers into the forests. In the Vilna Ghetto as in the Kovno Ghetto there were those who believed that if they must die, it was best to die together. And as Abba helped to lead people from the ghetto, he knew that if discovered he would be putting entire families at risk of reprisal by the Germans. Though it is not generally known, Abba had to make the excruciating decision to leave his own mother behind in the Vilna Ghetto. He told me once: "What does one say to the words that were used to say the Holocaust? One takes the words into his arms and rocks them and says, 'Don't cry, words. Don't cry.'"

It is strange to think of the quirks of fate that bring us to these terrible places—how Abba, born in the Crimea, as his family was on the way to Palestine from Lithuania and unable to continue because of the outbreak of World War I, ended up back in Vilna. Or the horrific fate of my relative David Wolpe, who had left Lithuania for good, or so he

Abba Kovner, Vitka Kempner, and UPO Group

David Wolpe

thought, to make *aliyah* to Palestine. After taking part in a demonstration there, he was imprisoned and sent back to Lithuania, just in time for the Soviet occupation and then the German occupation in 1941. From the Kovno Ghetto he was taken to Dachau Concentration Camp.

5

The Greeks call the day of the week that we name Friday, *Paraskevi*, preparation. Everything in my life prepared me for Lithuania. Whether as a small child coming home from school one day to find my parents sitting in stunned silence halfway up the stairs. Or in the southern Sahara Desert among the final habitations of Jews. Or climbing down beneath the earth into the vaulted bell caves of Bet Guvrin, used at times of

Josvainiai, Wolpe gravestone

danger to store arms or for hiding. Or in the Columbarium cave with its hundreds of alcoves for doves. Or in my Lithuanian grandmother's kitchen, watching her pluck feathers from chickens, seeing the golden eggs like moons inside the bodies of these birds. Or in the home of Greeks where I lived for two years, cooking and cleaning and caring for our children together until I owned the language. Or in a Greek village, high up in a mountain where the sounds of the bells of goats echoed along the stony paths and outcroppings, the goatherd in his fold below in the valley. Or at the end of summer gathering in the olive harvest, the village elder taking me under his wing, teaching me how the spring waters are released from the mountain top for each family, picking fresh leaves of *vlita* for the next meal, stuffing squash blossoms with rice and fresh herbs, and telling me about the Italian and German occupations, how the village was starved and one-third died.

What kind of preparation would this be? Something familiar. Something about the secrets written into the landscape. Something about villagers. For it was in villages of Lithuania that my family lived. Poor. Farmers. Married to the land. Small wooden houses without running water or electricity, gardens for growing vegetables and flowers, dough rising, butter in a churn. An apple tree behind a house in Dotnuva planted by members of my family before the war. Near the remains of a wooden barn. A Wolpe gravestone in Josvainiai. In the same village where American poet Stanley Kunitz's mother—a member of our family—was born. Quite late in her life at her son's urging, she wrote about the place where she was born:

> Without my consent I was brought into the world in the year 1866 much too early and in the wrong place as if I had any choice in the matter. It was a God-forsaken village of three hundred families in Lithuania in the province of Kovno. My name at birth was Yetta Helen Jaspon. We were one of about a hundred Jewish families in Yashwen (today Josvainiai). The rest of the population consisted of Lithuanians, Poles, with a sprinkling of Germans.
>
> My father was a descendant of Sephardic Jews who had left Spain in the sixteenth century. He and his family were

proud of their Spanish origin. In fact, their adopted surname Jasspon, in Russian "Yaspan" means "I'm Spanish." Ever since I can remember he was in poor health, as the result of an incident that happened before I was born, when he was strung from a tree by a band of Polish troopers during a pogrom and almost died of hanging before he was rescued. If my mother had not appeared on the scene, waving a letter of safe conduct from Count Radziwill, he would surely have perished. At that time the Poles and the Russians were fighting for possession of the land. My father was caught in the middle, since he was a grain merchant, whose chief customers were army horses, regardless of their nationality. He also owned several lime pits, which were under contract to the Russian government for use in the construction of buildings and railroads. He was a learned man, who loved to give orders, and his orders were law. We all feared our lord and master and would never dare to contradict or disobey him. He had come to Yashwen from Vilna in 1846 to marry my mother's oldest sister, who died six years later, leaving him one daughter. A year or so later he married my mother, who bore him five children, of whom I was the fourth.

My mother's family, named Wolpe [author's maternal family name], had lived in Yashwen for six or seven generations; she and I were both born in the same house. The Wolpes were a large clan, who had settled all over Poland and near the German border. My great-great grandfather on my mother's side was reputed to be the wisest man of his time. He was very pious and could perform miracles. People came from miles around to receive his blessing. As for his miracles, the only one that ever convinced me was that he lived to the age of a hundred and one....

When I was twelve years old I read Spinoza in my father's library and I lost my God. Spinoza did not deny the existence of God, but he destroyed my faith in a personal divinity. Whatever adversity befalls us is either the result of our own fault or that of others. Of all the troubles I've had since my childhood, I've always blamed myself for my misfortune because I could not believe it was God's will.[3]

Stanley Kunitz's mother left Eastern Europe in 1890 and arrived in America and never looked back.

Josvainiai, Babtai, Krak, Dotnuva, Ruseiniai, Rasein, Ariogala, Girtigola, Keidan, Baisigola, Ponevezh, Shadova, Šiauliai, Telz, Utian, Varzhan, Vandziogala, Vilkomir/Ukmerge, Vilna, Yanova, Kovno, Vilijampolė. These are the names of the villages and towns and cities where my family once lived. And in these same towns, where those who could not escape were killed.

A marker in a graveyard announces a village where my grandfather Meyer Aaron Wolpe was born and his father Eliezer Semach Wolpe before him—Ruseiniai. A scrap of paper in an archive—a conscription notice for my grandfather to join the Czarist army. He had already vanished and was somewhere in America, in West Virginia, a peddler with a cart and horse, praying in the barns of farmers, who likely thought it strange, a bearded man with *tfillin,* black leather straps wound around his arm, a tiny black box protruding from his forehead.

If there are enough pieces, memory can make of the scraps a story, a map. And sometimes, if one is lucky, more of the story comes into the light. Like the letter that explained what the child had seen in the faces of her parents that day in 1941 when the majority of the killing had already taken place.

6

We say Survivor. We say Rescuer. Collaborator. Witness. Perpetrator. Murderer. Survivor Sam Schalkowsky observes that we make categories. We draw sharp lines around each one. As if doing so makes this more palatable. Partitions. Once categorized, we can easily fit each candidate into its box. But some who rescued were criminals of the worst sort. Some who killed and betrayed were kindly, thoughtful of their own children. One could shoot in this moment, and save in the next. Obershaffer Fischer of the SS in Kaiserwald Concentration Camp, where Schalkowsky was imprisoned, was a pathological criminal of the worst sort, but could offer water to an elderly woman who was thirsty as she was being deported. Was he humane after all? Or does this mean that he understood what it meant to feel empathy for another human being despite his brutality the majority of the time? And does this make him therefore the worst kind of criminal because he knew the difference?

A sewer worker in Lodz, Poland who initially was paid to provide food and water to families hiding in the sewers underneath Lodz, continued this work when the money ran out, unlike others who helped initially and abandoned those in hiding when they were no longer paid to do so. This particular man was known to have served prison time for offenses related to robbery; yet he must be considered among the righteous for his behavior during the war. And when one of the children in the family could no longer live under the conditions in the sewer, and refused to eat or drink, he crawled with her through the sewer tunnel to a place where a manhole cover permitted rays of light to penetrate the darkness. He told her that someday she would be up there in that light, playing with other children, but for now she must eat and drink. And so she did. And she did survive.[4] In which category would you place such a man? There was nothing in his life previously that would

Yudel Ronder

indicate the kind of behavior he exhibited in the dank, rat-infested sewers of Lodz, no hint of bravery or willingness to risk his life. He was known as a common criminal. In the annals of humanity toward others, he is a shining example.

Yudel Ronder, born in Keidan (Kėdainiai) and serving in the 16th Lithuanian Regiment in Soviet Russia during the war, makes a distinction between two groups of rescuers: those who rescued Jews during the hardest times and those who took part in actions against the Jews or did nothing to prevent them and at the very end sought to make good in order to ease their consciences. "Knowing that some ninety-four percent or more of the Jews were massacred, I was interested in the three to six percent who were saved and how," Ronder says. He refers to knowing approximately one hundred families who saved Jews. "Some who saved Jews have not wanted to come forth to tell about this. Others claim to have saved Jewish lives but in fact did not."[5] In one case a man ascribed a neighbor's act of saving a Jewish woman as his own. After Ronder located the woman now living in St. Petersburg, Russia, who told him who actually had helped her, she stated that she had never heard of this man. When Ronder proposed that the man contact the woman, he disappeared.

Ronder describes a poor family in Kaišiadorys that saved ten Jews. After the war a forester came and killed the man who had saved Jews. Another woman claimed that her husband had rescued Jews, when in actuality her husband, a policeman, had been an active killer. Later, he helped one Jew. He had killed many Jews in 1941. One Jewish man had been saved by more than twenty different families. Ronder provided a number of examples of the Righteous and also listed those to be honored at Yad Vashem. As of January 1, 2018, 893 Lithuanians have been designated as Righteous Among the Nations for their heroic deeds in saving Jewish people in Lithuania.

Clearly, the designation of categories is an attempt to make sense of what is essentially unfathomable, to gain some mastery over a situation where the normal boundaries of behavior have collapsed. As spectators after the fact, perhaps this does provide a way to at least begin to examine behavior when the usual social norms have failed. But it is essential to understand that to do so is more for our benefit than for looking frontally into the abyss.

7

Certain interchangeable names were used and are understood differently, depending on who uses them. To cite a few: Shaulists, Forest Partisans, Forest Brothers, White Armbands/ Weissbindentragern, Bandits/Banditen, Self-DefenseGroups/Selbstverteidgungstruppen, local police, members of the TDA (National Labor Guard), auxiliary police battalions (under Nazi control), Lithuanian Activist Front/LAF.[6] The LAF was established in November 1940 by exiled representatives of the political parties in Lithuania who had escaped to Germany when the Soviets occupied the country. The LAF had underground branches inside Lithuania where they disseminated vicious anti-Semitic propaganda through leaflets smuggled into the country. The leaflets called for a popular rising if Germany attacked the Soviet Union and the elimination, by whatever means, of the Jews from Lithuanian soil. One of the LAF leaflets, headed "What are the Activists Fighting for?" stated that "the Lithuanian Activist Front, by restoring new Lithuania, is determined to carry out an immediate and fundamental purging of the Lithuanian nation and its land of Jews, parasites, and monsters. . . . [This] will be one of the most essential preconditions for starting a new life."[7]

8

In what language is memory embedded? Does it matter if a survivor tells her memories in the language of her adopted country, or in the language of her birth, or in the tongue she learned in hiding? Will the survivor remember events and feelings differently depending on the language in which these are told? More often than not, survivors were multilingual and being so in some cases saved their lives. Krystyna Chiger, who survived the Holocaust by hiding in the sewers beneath Lvov, Poland, for fourteen months, describes the torturous process through which memory passes. "My memories come to me in Polish. I think in Polish, dream in Polish, remember in Polish. Then it passes through Hebrew and somehow comes out in English. I do not know how this works, but this is how it is. Sometimes it has to go through German and Yiddish before I am able to tell it or understand it. All these thoughts. All these moments. All these sights and sounds and smells—tiny, fractured pieces, fighting for my attention, calling me to make sense of the whole."[8]

How does the language of extremity affect memory? What is memory's effect on language? Why does one survivor, fluent in many languages which she remembers to this day, have absolutely no memory of Lithuanian? And another, a man who hears Jews being taken to be killed in the next room, considers Lithuanian the agent of death and can no longer remember it? In which language does memory deliver its most vivid images—in the language of the senses, in the translations into language of extreme fear or heightened awareness, in the language of vigilance required for survival? And does vigilance, by necessity, rule out background context? "What do you remember?" a woman is asked who has been held up at knifepoint by three men in the vestibule of her apartment house. "The knife," she answers.

Chapter II

Versions

It's not the echo of bullets at the edge of the forest,
it is a swarm of silver bees
on the way to the hive of our orchard.

—Algimantas Mackus

1

If we could rewrite history, we would do as Lithuanian poet Algimantas Mackus instructs us: we would transform bullets into living creatures, used not to destroy life but to propagate it. Perhaps that wish is behind the great variety of historical "truths" that have emerged in Lithuania since World War II with regard to the deaths of Lithuania's Jewish population. The majority were killed during the opening months of the German occupation in 1941. The killing was said to have been done by Germans with Lithuanian collaborators, or by Lithuanians at the instigation of the Germans, or orchestrated by the Germans even before their arrival in Lithuania, or to avenge Jewish sympathizers during the previous Soviet occupation—1940–41—when Lithuanians were exiled to Siberia. Saulius Sužiedėlis, in "The Burden of 1941," writes that

> how we imagine the past is an important, perhaps even the most decisive, catalyst in the formation of collective identity, especially national consciousness. In as much as the purpose of commemoration, the affirmation of a particular vision of a shared history, is the reinforcement of group loyalty, the

exercise of the various solemn national remembrances is, at heart, a political act. By its very nature, the act of remembrance is hostile to critical analysis—shades of gray are unwelcome. This is particularly true of historical events characterized by mass violence. Wars, revolutions and genocides have winners as well as losers, perpetrators as well as victims, and it is natural that irreconcilable memories will clash.[1]

Since this exploration began its journey, much has changed in Lithuania. Initially, in 1991 after the long silence under communism, the "party line" regarding wartime activities had not quite made its way to the rural villages. Those who were willing to talk did not offer reasons for the murders which had taken place in every small hamlet, but they could describe the events:

> The Jews were taken to the church, locked up without food or water. I was a widow with two small children. I took food and water to them. I was locked up with them but I pleaded to be released. They did nothing wrong. At first they were taken at night so we would not see. To the forest where they were shot. Later, when no one spoke up, the killers became more courageous and took them in daylight.[2]

Now information about the Holocaust is being taught in the schools and through public international conferences, newspaper articles, museum exhibitions, films, book publications, educational projects. A national task force has been established to provide a program for Holocaust Remembrance, Education, and Research. Publications that have resulted from the work of the International Commission for the Evaluation of the Crimes of the Nazi and Soviet Occupation Regimes in Lithuania include: *The Preconditions for the Holocaust: Anti-Semitism in Lithuania* (2004); *Murders of the Prisoners of War and of Civilian Population in Lithuania* (2005); and *The Persecution and Mass Murder of Lithuanian Jews during Sumer and Fall of 1941* (2006). The Holocaust in Lithuania is no longer a secret, though its causes are still strongly debated, as is the issue of responsibility, and "not a single person who collaborated with the

Nazis has been convicted in independent Lithuania," according to Irena Veisaitė, former director of the Open Society Foundation in Lithuania.³

2

In this work, two main streams have emerged. The first has to do with multiple versions and perceptions of the same events. It is based on memories told during and immediately after the war and memories told approximately forty to fifty years after events took place and, in some cases, as written memoirs. Interviewees were from villages and cities, as well as Displaced Persons camps, and included survivors, witnesses, rescuers, collaborators, and murderers. Some testimonies were provided from those born after the war who now live in the United States and other countries.

The second part of the study has to do with the application of what is now known in neuroscience about the construction of memory to the study of Holocaust testimony, and to determine whether this approach can shed any new light on traumatic experience and the narrative and nature of memory. The reliability of traumatic memory is an issue of considerable controversy and importance, as is understanding how the synthesis of incoming information with preexisting information takes place. This study explores specific cognitive and affective issues having to do with the modulation of incoming stimuli and the formation of memory during trauma. For instance, researchers have observed that traumatic memories often do not initially have a narrative or sequential story but occur as sensations—auditory, visual, or affective. And even after a person creates a narrative in order to tell what he has experienced, when the memory reoccurs, it comes back piecemeal, as it had originally, sometimes as charged affect without being attached to a specific incident, sometimes as an auditory memory without a visual component.

One important question that arises in this work is the degree to which this inability to process and integrate information interferes with such processing and integration of nontraumatic experience later in life. One interviewee has spoken of "the modification of the gate," the effort to curtail what is taken in, even in nontraumatic situations (S.S.). Another has described the difficulty as he has grown older in seeing films about the Holocaust or visiting museum exhibits about the Holocaust, as if a prior working defense system has grown porous and resulted in a renewed vulnerability.[4]

3

What relevance has this work to the present? The Holocaust took place more than seventy years ago. What may be learned has relevance not only for elucidating the past but for those exposed to war and atrocity today, most importantly for children all over the world whose daily diet of trauma and violence in new forms and old continues in places such as the Sudan, Darfur, Iraq, Afghanistan, Syria. The work has important implications for the understanding and treatment of those in current days caught in war, imprisonment, exile, and forced to live under subhuman conditions. As Robert Kraft points out in *Memory Perceived: Recalling the Holocaust*, survivors of the Holocaust have dichotomous selves, the self during the extended trauma of the Holocaust, and the reconstructed self following the Holocaust—the one who has established new memories, new life experiences, new relationships.[5] Though the active life following the Holocaust—marriage, children, employment—is full and relatively happy, the Holocaust life in many cases does not diminish. It endures, waiting to be heard and seen and felt at any moment.

A paratrooper, now home from Iraq and suffering post-traumatic stress disorder, describes it this way: "It's like I can never come home. The war will never leave me; I will never leave the war."[6] Another soldier, home on leave from Iraq, goes to a shopping mall with his family and finds himself astonished that no one is guarding the entrances or exits to the mall. The vigilance, essential to survival in a wartime situation in Iraq, cannot be turned off in a situation where it is no longer necessary.

Thus, understanding the particular forms of trauma experienced during the Holocaust and their neurobiological components has application today for those who have suffered during the war in Iraq, to those who have survived genocide in the Sudan, to those imprisoned in Iran, to the murder of innocents in Syria. A young woman held captive in

Iran for eight years, with months in a particularly brutal and insidious punishment—being forced to sit in a "coffin" for fifteen hours at a time without moving and in total isolation—describes at first attempting to isolate herself completely from the experience. However, she later discovers that if she is to survive, she requires signs of life in the world, even the sounds in the distance of her captors, even watching a mosquito as it fills with her blood, a fly, the smallest emblem of life. She is horrified to discover that she can summon only two images from her previous life. At one point she thinks: Why not relax into madness? Why not just let go? But some resilience asserted itself. And she survived what many could not.[7] As she recounts her experience, it is as if she is in that prison, not remembering it from the safety of freedom.

A quite literal example is that of one whose reality from earliest memory was that of a rat-infested sewer, dank, filthy, with rank odors and the constant danger of drowning and perhaps above all, sensory deprivation. The child lived under these conditions for fourteen months. His identity and conception of home and family was formed under these conditions. Imagine, then—if it were even possible—what it was like when the child was suddenly liberated from his hiding place. When one has lived in darkness for a time, it is not possible to immediately see in the normal sense. The child, pulled through the manhole to freedom "screamed in terror. . . . He shouted, 'I want to go back! I want to go back!'" At a certain point, he even attempted to climb back down into the sewer.[8]

Perhaps the trauma of the child can shed light on the conflict soldiers feel about which identity they belong to, protecting the lives of the men in their battalion, attempting to stay alive themselves, carrying out the mission they have been assigned, or embracing relationships and their former lives when they are no longer on the battlefield. We might ask if the life in the dark, the life in war ever really diminishes. And we must ask how it reasserts itself in a life where extreme vigilance and the alteration of identity are no longer necessary.

4

In sum, the partitions that have been erected between disciplines are giving way. Psychoanalytic theory is being examined in light of neuroscience.

Molecular biologists are teamed with bioengineers, physicists, and biochemists to provide insights about immunology. The tools of immunology are being applied to the study of consciousness. We no longer think of memory as a vast immutable library housed in our gray matter which preserves a literal representation of the world, but rather as a dynamic process calling upon multiple areas and systems in the brain. This project attempts to link current thinking in the neurosciences about memory formation with Holocaust testimony taken in recent days as well as testimony from those who, because of the relative isolation of Lithuania, harbored memories and conceptions that went unchallenged during the period following World War II, untested by discussion with others or by any national source of information about the past. Such experiences and internal narratives evolved in a walled-off place and surfaced as they must have existed during the war and prior to it. This project attempts to bring a complex set of approaches to bear on a core issue. What can we learn about how memory is encoded, stored, and retrieved under the extreme circumstances of the Holocaust?

Chapter III

OUT OF SIGHT

1

I have been haunted by a small poem, "To My Brother Miguel in Memoriam," by the Peruvian poet Cesar Vallejo, which concludes this way:

> Miguel, you hid yourself
> one night in August, nearly at daybreak,
> but instead of laughing when you hid, you were sad.
> And your other heart of those dead afternoons
> is tired of looking and not finding you. And now
> shadows fall on the soul.
> Listen, brother, don't be too late
> coming out. All right? Mama might worry.

Embedded in the game of hide-and-seek, a game they had played in childhood, is the surviving brother's grief. But what was there about this particular game that it contained such deep resonance? As students in my undergraduate class were discussing the poem, I was reminded of the developmental period when babies will be transformed from contented responsive states to howling grief the moment the mother steps out of sight. They are unable to generalize sufficiently, to know that the mother will come in from the distance in a moment, that she is not gone forever.

Eventually the little one—and each of us—learns to postpone the need for her continual presence because we come to understand that she will come and go, but,if we are lucky enough, she will always return. Our needs will be met. And eventually we will learn to take care of our own needs, when we are developmentally ready to do so.

Yet as I read this poem in the context of my students' discovering its many layers, I became aware of another resonance, another set of memories: the actual game of hide-and-seek and the strangely traumatic experiences associated with it. Many of us can remember playing this game. One child stands in a visible place, covers his eyes and counts to twenty while the others secrete themselves behind trees, under a layer of leaves, inside a thicket. When the counting is done, the counter seeks out the hidden children and the first one found becomes the counter. Sometimes the older children desert the counter and when he goes to find them, they are nowhere to be found. There is inherent danger in this game: The counter might, in his effort to locate the others, wander off and lose his way; a stranger might intercept the one hiding; a child might choose to hide near a stream or river bank and lose his footing.

In the context of this poem by Vallejo, I thought again about the disappearance of the mother. And how, in this poem, that game becomes the vehicle for the brother's expression of grief at the loss of his brother. That perhaps all along we are rehearsing for and recovering from the final loss, our final hiding place. "Listen, brother, don't be late/ coming out. All right? Mama might worry," says the surviving brother, as though at any moment his missing brother will magically appear. As though, for the sake of his mother's grief, the brother must appear and live. The wish is said in the voice of a child.

Perhaps it is this elemental need and fear that so governs our reading of the *Akedah*, the Binding of Isaac in *Genesis*. The boy, for reasons that are not clear to him, is taken off by his father to be sacrificed. For all intents and purposes, as far as we are told, the mother plays no role in this, has no awareness of what is about to happen, the very mother who had to wait until old age to conceive and bear this beloved child. That Isaac is spared does not reduce the trauma that even we, as readers, experience.

2

I have puzzled over the reluctance of survivors to share their experiences, those who served in resistance movements and those who survived concentration camps. In some cases, I have been told that though they wished to talk about what had happened to them with family members after the war, they were advised that it was best to get on with their lives and not to dwell in the past. Others have adamantly refused to speak of their experiences, whether to those close to them or for archival purposes in order to leave an historical legacy. At times, quite late in their lives, some have elected to be interviewed. This reluctance has been true of some perpetrators as well who only recently have been willing to be interviewed.

Harvey Peskin, in "From Transmitting to Transmuting Holocaust Trauma: A Psychotherapist's View," points out that

> liberation from the camps did not so simply liberate the survivor's mind to bear witness to the past—to know and be seen knowing. Not to be seen seeing was elemental in the psychotic, non-communicating universe of death camps and concentration camps where moment to moment survival clung desperately to concentrated nondisclosure and nonwitness—in short, to invisibility. . . . For many, surviving Nazi atrocity yielded a suspended state—neither enslavement nor liberation—that remained contaminated by the persecutor's injunction against survivors bearing witness to the very criminal acts which they survived.[1]

Further, Peskin notes the "remarkable inventiveness" by which the Nazis "corrupted innocence by supplanting victims' blamelessness with complicity and collaboration." After liberation, the survivor was not yet able to separate the "perversion of these affects from any integrated position of appraisal, acknowledgment, and meaning."

A student who had returned from active duty during the Vietnam War had been totally silent about his experiences there until we commenced the study of Dante's *Inferno*. Oddly, it was Dante to whom he first bore witness. The descent into the underworld provided him a framework for his own descent into the underworld of violence and death and into the hidden cache of memory that resided within him. When he asked that I read something he had written, I had no idea of any of his experience nor of the singular gift and responsibility I had been handed. Even today it terrifies me to think of how easily I might have unwittingly scared this offering away. Late that night I opened the packet of papers to see that Dante had provided him a vehicle to gain access to his experience, to begin to own it outright—that he had been rescued from a ring of fire by a helicopter, that he had been in a special reconnaissance unit that went ahead of the troops, that all of his men had been killed, that he could spot a trip wire thread to explosives as fine as a hair, that he had never stopped this kind of vigilance so necessary for survival in Vietnam. And I began to understand his behavior as we waited outside the classroom for the preceding class to finish, how he always stood at the far end of the hall as close to the stairway and an escape route as possible, how Vietnam was here with him at all times.

What Dante—with his leopards of malice and his dark ledges swept by whirlwinds, and a forlorn figure who bears his head as a lamp in his hand—had to offer this young man was the safety of a place that was commensurate with his pain and suffering, with the depth of what he experienced in his wartime life, yet a place that would not further endanger him. And that step permitted the next one—placing into the hands of another human being the first words born of memory, a sacred trust.

3

And as for the literal hiding, Rabbi Ephraim Oshry in *The Annihilation of Lithuanian Jewry* writes:

> Where did people hide? The question should be: Where didn't they hide? In walls, under houses, in chimneys, in the depths of the sewage system. Wherever imagination suggested that one's body would not be visible, that is where people hid. People sought places where no one would ever imagine that a person could hide.[2]

Even the body seemed too large, too visible. " 'If I were smaller, I'd fit into this hole.' People walked around shrunken, afraid of their own shadows. Their hands were too long, their legs too thick."³

The hiding places were given the name *malina,* a word whose origin has to do with a robber's cache, the goods he has stolen, the literal translation, "raspberry." And later, at times daughters were given this name. A replica of a *malina* has been constructed in the attic of the Vilna Gaon Jewish State Museum in Lithuania by one of the Austrian Gedenkdienst volunteers.

Ephraim Sten,⁴ born in the town of Zloczow, Poland, and in hiding during World War II for three years beginning when he was thirteen, did eventually return to Zloczow. In a sense, he had been returning for years. In memory: "A German officer, tall polished boots, his gun pointed at a big-eared boy in short pants. The boy is running into an alley. On the right, a rough clapboard fence." And in the physical reality: ". . . how nice to find the fence still standing, as if remembering my athletic feat." He kept a journal during the war years. As an adult in Israel in the 1970s—because his children wanted to see his diary—he began to translate the diary from Polish to Hebrew. And in the course of this work, the adult began to respond to the entries he had made as a youngster. Parts of the journal were faded, parts torn and crumbling. Sten cut away the faded parts and glued what remained to clean pages. What we have is a remarkable double testimony—the adult reaching back across the years of his life to the boy he had been to create a dialogue.

The adult is hard on the boy he was; yet the boy speaks of having only one asset: "exaggerated self-criticism." The boy who speaks from these pages is astonishingly learned, fully conscious, his observations unique: "Jews have always been liquidated. . . . Who are we anyway? A comma in History." He muses on the terrible irony that Chmielnicki exists in history because of the "thousands of Jewish and Polish victims that he slaughtered. . . . Hitler, too, will enter History because of us." And the adult is equally critical of his own motivations. The diary, he writes, "is supposed to remind one of that cliché . . . about the phoenix rising from its ashes. What becomes clearer and clearer in this writing is that the ashes are the end. . . . The writing was supposed to be a contribution to memory, recycling a dark period in life, but in retrospect I'm convinced it was born by mistake. For decades, I was not conscious of the load crushing my soul. This damned writing has newly rediscovered everything." The actual return to Zloczow gives credence to the fact that the boy had once lived in that place, that the adult hadn't invented it, and writing about this, the adult becomes real to himself and to the possibility that some "trace" of him will remain.

The Polish poet Tadeusz Rozewicz once wrote: "Forget about us/ about our generation/ live like human beings/forget about us/we envied/ plants and stones/we envied dogs." Ephraim Sten, in his journal written between the years 1941 and 1944, speaks of envying the chickens in the yard their freedom, or the dog he embraces who "smells of fields, forest, wind." As an adult, he speaks of the Tel Aviv he loves, for knowing that at any moment he can go out, "enter anywhere" he wishes. Here, he sympathizes with Anne Frank, "the girl imprisoned in her room, unable to move about, bereft of Man's basic right: Freedom." He tells of the terrible passivity required during hiding: "in a grave-like pit, narrow and long, eight people locked into a small space, in pairs, without being able to speak for many hours at a time—boredom, darkness, hunger." Germans living virtually in the next room in the same house.

There comes a moment, after an altercation among those living so closely together, when Sten contemplates leaving, simply walking away. "When I was a child I saw a man drowning. He was swimming in the river and suddenly it seemed somebody was pulling him by his leg. He waved his arms, he might have cried out, and then disappeared in the deep." The adult Sten acknowledges that this memory likely indicates that had he actually left, he would have been killed. He jokes then about the "terrific posthumous finish to [his] diary." Plays, translations, royalties. But alas—the money wouldn't flow into his pockets because he hadn't any pockets!

In dreaming, the role of the body is stillness, while the role of the dreamer is to wander about in the world, backward and forward through time with no limitation. In hiding, the body like that of the dreamer's must be completely still; yet the mind of the hidden one is acutely attentive, vigilant for any sound that could result in his discovery and death.

Vamik D. Volkan, in "After the Violence," writes about "perennial mourning" where those who have suffered trauma postpone completion of the mourning process. They employ what he terms *linking objects,* "a mental meeting point between representation of the deceased and the corresponding self-image of the mourner," a letter, a piece of clothing, a watch. Though linking objects can be used to postpone the mourning process, they can also be used adaptively to initiate future mourning when the mourner has the emotional resources to confront the loss. The small journal kept by Ephraim Sten during his years in hiding, replete with intricate architectural drawings, became such a linking object. It forms the basis for the dialogue between the adult and the child he had once been. And it has taken the better part of a lifetime for its author to achieve any semblance of wholeness.

Eli Wiesel once said that when the voice of the child he had been before the war coalesces with the voice of the man he is now, he begins to hear the first words of his novels. What has been vanquished is his adolescence. Across the chasm of the Holocaust, the man meets once more the child he was. Together, united, integrated, the man can begin to speak. Near the end of his journal, Ephraim Sten writes:

> In the epic of his wanderings Ulysses once sat at the entrance of the Underworld and waited for the soul of his departed friend. He had a slaughtered ram at his feet because its fresh blood had the virtue of reviving consciousness. Around him swirled and pushed multitudes of the dead who also wanted to gain a moment of resurrection. But Ulysses was determined not to let them approach. He arrived from far away and was waiting for only one soul.
>
> In this writing I am both Ulysses and the slaughtered ram. My own blood revived several ghosts and like Ulysses I kept my right to choose. The ghosts that were no part of the diary crowded round my puddle of blood, but I spurned them and didn't let them have another transformation. That was my privilege, as in Homer's metaphor, of emotional and intellectual choice. Possibly the others' turns would have arrived if I had allotted myself enough time. But now I'm bidding farewell to the voices, faces and images to which I haven't brought life but my dreams were overflowing with them for a long time.[5]

4

The buried identities which later come to haunt their owners and their progeny were sometimes never resolved. Even in the heroic acts of saving children by those brave enough to take the risk, the shadow of earlier parents and identities, of lives lived elsewhere and differently, hovered over the lives of the young ones fortunate enough to live. Reading Shira Nayman's fiction collection *Awake in the Dark*[6] took me back to an icy November day in 1996 in the village of Punija (Punia), adjacent to Butrimonys and Alytus, where some 65,000 Jews had been murdered during World War II. It was a day of memorial and reconciliation. Jewish children and adults from Vilnius and Kaunas joined with those in the villages and the priests from Punija, walking the long walk across a bridge, going first to the Jewish cemetery where *kaddish* was recited and where the children placed candles at the graves, and then attending a service in the Catholic church where a menorah had been placed on the altar. Later, the children danced and sang Hebrew melodies and later still, in an unheated room, there was a reception. A woman came up to me to talk and I asked her why she had come to this occasion. "Perhaps, "she said, "I too am Jewish and don't know it." How many children were taken into Lithuanian families, made to erase their language, identities, their very names? Some found out the truth later. Others never did. And of those who learned the truth, some chose to continue as they had, as Catholic Lithuanians, remaining in their villages, while others searched for the full story of their lives, whatever of it could be reclaimed.

Nayman, a clinical psychologist, chronicles the split identities of those raised believing that their lives have taken a certain course, like any of us, but having fragments of memories or disruptions that would say otherwise.[7] In story after story this nagging doubt emerges, as if at any moment a small seam could give way and tremors of an impending earthquake open the life wide and put the lie to all that a character believed to be the truth of her existence.

The author uses a narrative structural device that reinforces the sense of these broken identities—sections separated by time, location, and by narrator. For instance, in "The Lamp," the daughter, offspring of her Jewish mother and a Nazi officer, alternates telling her versions of events with those of her mother from locations in Dresden and in New York, during the war and in the present.⁸ The effect is to place a similar burden upon the reader as exists in the characters of the stories—to integrate disparate and traumatic experience. And, at times, unknowable experience.

In "Dark Urgings of the Blood," a psychiatrist and her patient appear initially as individuated but eventually merge as their histories seem to be identical.⁹ The psychiatrist asks: "Is this how a madman feels? Convinced that the impossible parameters of his vision—everything coming together *just so*, everything filled with threat, and all of it pointed toward *me*—is the absolute and fundamental truth?" And later, after finally initiating the questioning of her father, she says: "I think about my mother's principle: *No trespassing.* I feel a shock of shame . . . I want to . . . go back to the unruffled existence I led . . . to allow my father . . . to remain in the careful chamber he has made of his life, the past safely sealed away."

The narrators of these stories dare to cross the forbidden threshold, dare to open the past, no matter the consequences. These are courageous stories about women who must find a way, once they have unmanned the schizophrenic division of their lives, to reintegrate the parts of their lives. They must face the taboo of breaking apart the parental marriage that has been based on agreed-upon silence about the past, allowing hideous secrets to come streaming out. Whether in breaking through a wall for the hidden message or breaking the lock on a metal box, the stories teach us about the dangers of secrets and the raw courage that it takes to bring the past into the light of the present.

5

When I was a child in America I learned early that when traveling on the streetcar or walking in the streets of Baltimore, it was better to turn my Hebrew books over in such a way that others passing by wouldn't notice the Hebrew letters. Such was a child's perception of the need to hide her Jewishness in a time of overt anti-Semitism. Nor did I understand a beating by an older boy on the earth of the schoolyard, shouting "Jew,

Jew!" when I was too young to know what it meant to be Jewish. Even today, after all of these years, without thinking about it, this desire to hide any emblem of my religion is still alive, though I do not abide it. And surely in those early days, I would not have died of my Jewishness. A compliment then that one did not look Jewish was tinged with irony and sadness. Then to imagine how it was for those caught in underground bunkers in Kovno, how children growing up in a climate where their main vocation was to become invisible, that their lives depended upon how small and blank they could be, ciphers, what bunker or hole in the earth or stairwell or sack they could hide in, blanking out family of origin, religion, even their primary language. And for those few who survived, to imagine how the lost self is recovered, reconstructed, when it has been taken during the critical period of identity formation. In some cases, the person has no memory of the family of origin if the child was young enough when taken into the home and life of rescuers. And even if the child was fortunate enough to remain with parents, this perception of self was severely altered.

Chapter IV

LEISER'S SONG

On June 15, 1940, the Soviet Union occupied Lithuania. A year later, on June 22, 1941, Nazi Germany broke its pact with the Soviets and invaded Lithuania. The Red Army fled. A killing rampage against Jews took place in more than two hundred villages. In my journeys there over twenty-five years, I have visited massacre pits in many villages and towns, some hidden in deep forest. The Jews of Kaunas, some thirty thousand, were ordered to move into the Kovno Ghetto in August 1941, an area that contained approximately seven thousand people in what is called Slobodka or Vilijampolė, across the river from Kaunas. It was here, in August 1941, that my cousin Leiser Wolpe, then a teenager, moved from his home on Laisvės Alėja, Kovno (Kaunas), with his pregnant mother into a stable. His father had been killed earlier by Lithuanians in the cellar of their apartment house in Kaunas.

In recent years I discovered, thanks to a physician friend who had known Leiser many years earlier, that he was alive and living in Zurich, Switzerland. Thus, a correspondence began that took place over nine years until his death. For the most part our conversations were by telephone, almost on a daily basis and often several times a day. His wife Ada, a painter, would write lengthy and beautiful letters.

What follows here are bits and scraps of our conversations, in no particular order, in the same way that his thoughts followed no logical order but were often interrupted by intrusive images, memories, avoidances, repetitions. Though I often had to hurry to keep up with his sudden shifts of thought, I had one distinct advantage. I had walked the places of his suffering many times. And by one of those strange

Leiser Wolpe

coincidences that life can offer, during my very first visit to Lithuania in 1993, a survivor of Keidan—the very town of Leiser's birth—walked with me describing the people who had once lived there.

    I did not know at the time that it was Leiser's birthplace, nor that many others of my family had lived there as well. I knew Leiser Wolpe's territory and landscape. I had, with survivors, walked the perimeter of the burial pit where many of our family had been murdered. I had walked through Vilijampolė, site of the former Kovno Ghetto where he and his mother managed to survive, in the company of those who had been imprisoned there as well. And I had walked those places alone, touching the buildings and the earth where so many perished. I talked to witnesses, rescuers, survivors, and to collaborators in those places. I did not go to Dachau, nor walk in the steps of his forced march. Nor to Stutthof Concentration Camp where his mother died. But perhaps it helped that he knew that what he told me was not abstract, but was palpable, because I had embodied the physical places and presences of the world he was sharing with me. I will always be grateful for his friendship and trust.

1

Friday fell off the calendar. Just at the moment when an old man was crossing Bahnhofstrasse in Zurich. The day fled the calm progression of days. He was carrying his parcel of food from Kaufmann's. He had only to reach Bahnhofplatz to find his tram stop and go home. Did he hear the approaching tram? He could not see it, his eyesight nearly gone. What did he think as he stood there in the path of the speeding tram? Did he imagine his small brother burning alive in a hospital in Vilijampolė? Did he remember then the tiny newborn infant brother born in the ghetto whom he'd had to bury when he was himself little more than a child? Did he see the face of his mother in Stutthof Concentration Camp? Or his father dying in his arms in the cellar at 78 Laisvės Alėja? Did he remember at that moment how he rose up from that cellar of death and tried to get help? How no one would open their doors to him? That?

Or did death cover him like a blanket, muffling thought, extinguishing memory? Was it like that? Or did he send a final message to the one who had been so kind to him? To Stephen? *Help me again.* Did he say that? Is that why Stephen noticed a small message on a local television station about an old man hit by a tram? Why he called the hospital, dreading what he might find out?

He calls. Three in the morning, his time. Nine in the evening, mine. He calls back. He's dressed. He's having tea. Soon he will leave his apartment. I, on the other hand, will go to sleep. My night is beginning. *Have a good morning,* I tell him. *Have a good rest,* he tells me. And then, *Cheerio!* And then a few more quietly told goodbyes. It is hard for him to hang up.

He seldom sleeps. Sometimes he lies down for an hour or two. *Did you sleep when you were a little boy?* I asked him. *Oh, it wasn't like that,* he answered. I've made him go there again. I hadn't meant to do that. I must be more careful next time. *After the war, I would have terrible nightmares. Ada was afraid the neighbors would complain. I would call out. I would scream. In St. Ottilien I was too sick to cry out. They put ice on my chest to stop the bleeding. In Gautien, when the nun named Innocent took care of me, I was too sick to cry out. But later.*

I thought I would go to the police station. So I would have somebody to talk to, he tells me. He has changed the subject again. *I don't think that's a good idea,* I tell him, concerned that a visit to the police in the early morning hours might result in a longer stay than he intends. Now he calls me two times a day.

On this day, the ninth day of July, he will be buried. The man who never slept will have eternal sleep. There, in the cemetery with his beloved Ada. Companion artist who painted the shadows out of his life. *I painted him in the garden at Tessin, there among the flowers and trees. But there was only the sun, brightness and color,* she wrote to me once.[1] He told me that he couldn't have lived had he not met her. *She was a veil between me and the Holocaust.* That's how he put it.

But perhaps the man who never slept will wander through the nights of the afterlife as he wandered through them in life. At first I thought it was the nightmares he was afraid of. That all the details of his past, so critically intact, would suck him back into that mire of pain, torture's innovations imposed on him. But later I found out he was afraid of something altogether different.

I begged them not to sedate me, he told me, *when I was in the hospital. And why was that?* I asked him. *If one is in pain and cannot sleep, medication is usually given in hospitals. I did not know what I might do, what I was capable of. I could hurt someone. I might kill someone,* he told me.

He called me nine times yesterday. And left messages. They all ended with *Cheerio!* The last call was in the middle of the night his time. When Ada was alive, he would go into the kitchen and make jam at three in the morning.

Today I call him. *Leiser,* I begin. *What . . . what do you say?* He can't hear me. Sometimes I think he is listening so hard to what is going on inside his head that it's hard for anything from outside to penetrate. But maybe today he has forgotten to put his hearing aid in. Or perhaps it needs a new battery.

I need you to help me, I say. *What, what?* he asks. And in German: *Wie bitte? Bitte? I want to know how we are related,* I say, my voice getting louder and louder, sailing across the state of Maryland, rushing over the Chesapeake Bay, going east, all the time east, all the way to Zurich.

He hears me. At last. I can feel him listening. He begins slowly. He would rather tell me about how he ordered Joel Elkes's books from London, the book Elkes wrote about his father, Elchanan Elkes, who was head of the Ältestenrat in Kaunas during the Nazi occupation. Elkes who attempted to stop the murders of ten thousand Jews and was beaten nearly to death. Elkes who died in Dachau and wrote to his children: "Remember, both of you, what Amalek has done to us. Remember and never forget it all your days; and pass this memory as a sacred testament to future generations."

And now he remembers my question. *Do you think,* he begins, *that when we lived in Keidan we thought about family trees, about genealogy? About making a map of all the families? We thought about Shabbos. We thought about how will we be able to get a chicken for Shabbos. I was a little boy. I don't know.* We burst out laughing. We laugh and we laugh, the distance is swallowed up. We are in each other's arms laughing.

I've made a decision, he tells me, changing the subject again. *Adrian told me to get rid of everything. I look at all the things—paintings, drawings, jewelry, vases and carvings and Ada's brushes and paints.* I know before he goes on what he will say. *I will learn to paint,* he announces. Before Ada vanishes from inside him, he will take all those years when he watched her work, when he cooked for her, and stretched canvases, and carried her paintings and drawings from place to place, and he will turn into her. He will become a painter and she will be inside him, and his arms will move as she moved them. He will see the world through her eyes. And he will paint.

But a moment later he proclaims he must work: he has too much to do. He must prepare the exhibition of Ada's work. Not for December, but for spring.

Another subject, quite suddenly. I am not quite prepared for the next words. *Did you read the Joseph Roth book yet?* he asks me. He wants very badly for me to read that book. I ordered it from Canada because it is out of print in the United States. And because he told me to. I think I will find Leiser inside that book. That the poor beggar on the cover will turn into Leiser. I am saving the reading of it. I think I will find out something about Leiser that may frighten me. But there's nothing that can frighten me more than what I already know about him. Lying in the cellar of the apartment building among the dying men, lying in their bleeding. Lying in his father's blood. His younger brother burned alive in the hospital.

I came up from the cellar. There was a window you could look through into the yard. To see if the Lithuanians came back. The caretaker of the building said in Polish when he caught sight of me: "What! You are still alive! Go back to the cellar." He called the Lithuanians to get me. But I escaped. On the twenty-second of June, nineteen forty-one, the Germans came to Lithuania. The murders of my father and the other men took place on June twenty-seventh. I was wounded. On the first floor lived a family taken away. One man who was paralyzed remained with some small children. He didn't let me in. On the second floor, the family Kacerginski. They were too frightened to let me in. I ran to the third floor, the family Zacherkhan from Klaipėda with two girls, two nurses. Mr. Zacherkhan didn't take me. I walked back down, came to the first floor where the sick man lived, gave him a push, came in and locked the door. In the bathroom I took a towel to wipe up the blood on the floor and steps. They had some suitcases. I hid in a corner where they could not find me, took one coat from the cabinet. My coat had blood on it. Later I walked up to the Jewish Hospital. I could see the German soldiers taking groups of people away, but I was able to get to the hospital. Moshe Braun and another professor operated on me. After the war when the professor returned to Lithuania, he was arrested by the Russians. I left the hospital. My mother came back to Laisvės Alėja. On the twenty-eighth day of August, nineteen forty-one, we were closed into the Kovno Ghetto.

He is spelling again. "T" as in "torture," "A" as in "Aktion," "R" as in "round-up," "H" as in "Hitler." He laughs. He's still there, in the concentration camp, in the round-up, in the ghetto, still lying in the dark basement of his building among the dead and dying men, among them his own father. He's never come home, not really.

He's sitting in a restaurant having breakfast. He doesn't know what to do. He has a dilemma he can't solve. A boy, an American boy, for some reason, is photographing his food at the next table and inadvertently includes Leiser in the picture. When the boy realizes this, he steps over to Leiser's table to apologize. Leiser invites him to sit down with him. The boy is traveling, on a vacation. Somewhere, back a while, he's had a breakdown, but now he seems to have recovered enough to make this journey.

They end up spending the day together. Leiser, despite his age, walks the boy around Zurich. Joseph knows nothing about the Holocaust. He is about to get a complete lesson from the old man who takes him to the synagogue and to the cemetery where his recently dead wife is buried. He takes him to see art, the Chagall windows, to share a meal, and to the studio where Ada's paintings are stacked by the hundreds on the floor in every conceivable inch of space.

By the end of the day, they have become friends, the old man and this young boy. *I need you like a bodyguard,* Leiser tells Joseph.

Since Leiser died, I cannot sleep. I have taken his habit. No more than an hour or two at a time. I am become him. That shall be my way of mourning this time. Each death is different. So will I dream of his mother? Or his brother enveloped in flames? Or the small infant wrapped in a man's undershirt, and buried? I do dream. Of a purse. With identity papers. A missing purse. Perhaps it is to death we go. Without identity. No need then.

In the cemetery where Ada is buried, Leiser brings small stones to place on the matzevah. *Now it piles up like a little mountain,* he tells me. At first, he couldn't find stones in the graveyard to place on Ada's gravestone, for remembrance. So he bought stones at the market, twelve Swiss francs for three stones. It seemed strange to me that he had to buy stones, so I sent him a beautiful stone my son had given me a long while back. I wrapped it carefully and mailed it. I wanted Ada to have something from me.

When it arrived in Zurich, Leiser was afraid to open the package. *I will take it to the rabbi,* he told me. *Leiser,* I said, *please get the package and open it while we talk together on the phone. Wait a moment,* he says, putting the phone down and dropping it. Now he is back. *I have your picture here. When I talk to you on the telephone, I see your face,* he tells me. He is always saying we must meet again face to face. *Panim el panim,* I tell him. *Like Moses on Mount Sinai, face to face.* The only place in the entire Bible where God appears to a human being. But not like that, I think. Only a poor old man and an old woman attempting to be of help from a great distance.

Now he has the package. *Open it, Leiser!* I say. He opens it slowly as if it might go off, like a bomb. Inside the tissue paper, he takes out the beautiful tiny stone. The next day he takes it to the cemetery and puts it on Ada's grave. He tells me that some days later there was a terrible storm and all the little stones flew off. *Only my stone remained.*

I imagine Ada's grave with all the stones he's brought. He goes there nearly every day to talk with her, to receive her messages. But he needn't do that. He has only to open any of the hundreds of pages she has left for him in her journals and diaries and between the pages of their books. He could receive messages from Ada for a thousand years and they would not be depleted.

Today he has called seven times. Like seven lean years and seven plentiful ones, in Pharaoh's dream. The dream that Joseph interpreted. I call him this time. *Are you comfortable?* he asks. I don't know if he means if I am sitting down, if he has something terrible to tell me. *Your home, I mean,* he says. *Did you buy oil? I'm wearing a thin pullover and a tee-shirt,* he tells me. *Like a sauna! Don't stint to save money by not ordering oil,* he says. *I always kept it warm in the studio in Tessin for Ada. If she wasn't happy, she couldn't paint. Sometimes it would get so hot in the winter, she'd have to open the window. I would tell her—you see all the mountains; the beautiful landscape will always be there but we are going away.* I think of the ghetto stable where he helped his mother to give birth. I think of him in Dachau in winter.

The conversation the next day begins without preamble. It takes a moment for me to realize that Leiser is talking about Joseph. *I started to write to him. I didn't like to take any food. I made jam. I had a lot of plums. We had eaten plums. I had to rest. It is like homemade. I filled two glasses. You see what I wrote to him is in Yiddish. He will have to go to the rabbi.* Leiser bursts out laughing, trying to imagine how this kind young man will manage with this letter from him in Yiddish. The irony is that the rabbi in the main synagogue where this young man lives is also a cousin to Leiser. Leiser doesn't know about this.

Here is what he has written in the letter to Joseph: *"My dear Yossel, Yosele, Yoshke . . ."* We both laugh. Leiser has given this lovely young man the most affectionate of Jewish names, all the diminutive versions of Joseph in Yiddish. *Now I like that you can laugh,* he tells me. *I have a very bad conscience to tell you about the Holocaust.*

"In 1940," the letter continues, *"the Russians came into Lithuania and Jews were not allowed to write in Yiddish. You are like a star come from the heavens. Your whole life is before you. You are young. Your photograph is standing before me on the table. You have a nice expression on your face, ein Schmakel. Like the rays of the sun. That's the photo what you made. I hope you had a nice time in Rome and came home to your mama, sister, granny, girlfriend.*

"I went through fire. All is exploded in flames. I can shout. I can't pray because my life during the war got mixed up. A lot of members of my family are lying in a grave in Keidan, 2700 lying in the grave. Nineteen meters long, nine meters deep, nine meters wide. My brother Chaim was burned alive in the hospital in the small ghetto. Benjamin, my baby brother, lived only a few days after my mother gave birth. I brought him to the cemetery with an old man and wrapped him in an old shirt and buried him. My mama was killed in Stutthof Concentration Camp. My father was shot in front of me. I was lying under the dead people. I was the only one wounded and I could run away. The sadness is in me. And this is part of my life." Now Leiser stops reading and comments: *The rabbi will have a difficult time.* He laughs. *How will he translate this letter for Joseph?* They say that anger is the last defense before tears, but perhaps with Leiser it is laughter.

Now he has suddenly switched subjects again. *They couldn't digest it.* I hurry to catch up with his thought. Twenty-five-page letters he wrote after liberation. He was suffering from tuberculosis and was in a sanatorium in Davos, Switzerland, and had time to write down his experiences and thought. But his family in South Africa threw all the letters away.[2]

The next day Leiser continues reading his letter to Joseph: *"Monday, when you sat opposite me, your sunshine face was a miracle. Now it is getting cold. Soon will come snow. The snow makes the air clear and dry and very beautiful. When you came to Zurich . . ."* (*What does the rabbi do when he puts his two hands together?* he asks me. *A blessing,* I answer.) *"I bless you for that. What can I tell you more? It was so good to be with you. I have to be very strong. To remember you."* Here Leiser begins to cry. He is remembering Ada who has died. Perhaps he is remembering his little brother. And perhaps he is afraid he will never see this boy again. Perhaps this boy is the one he might have become in another life. *"And now,"* he continues, *you came on my road and maybe we can something do. It is great you are a born photographer."*

She—he speaks of his wife suddenly—*was a very great believer in being a nice person and she had a good heart and she said to me: You have to believe in the good of people. I couldn't. The letter is not finished,* he tells me. *I made my bed every day,* he says. *I don't like the meal we had together in the restaurant. It is a mass production. I said to Joseph, Come on into this shop. I took him to a shop to buy a little meat and vegetables to take away the bad taste of the other food.*

And so another day is coming to an end. I am only afraid that Leiser will never see Joseph again. He will be very disappointed. But for now, he will send a shawl to Joseph's granny, a lemon-colored one. And in a little while, around two in the morning, he will take a bath and lie down for an hour or two, the most he ever sleeps. And by four in the morning he will be wandering around again, receiving messages from his wife Ada, sorting through her papers, taking the washing down to the washing place where it has been accumulating for several weeks. And if he is lucky, a boy name Joseph from America will remember him and will one day return to Zurich. And if he is really lucky, this old man will be there to receive the boy.

What do I know about Leiser so far? I know that he takes a bath twice daily. Once in the morning—whatever his morning means. And once in the evening. I know that he goes to Germany to have his hair cut, even though he has hardly any hair. He tells me he does not like it to get long in the back, that it isn't clean. Perhaps in the ghetto and in the concentration camp first the hair was long and then it was shaved because of lice and to dehumanize, to make them anonymous. He often talks about money, about how much things cost, how much it would be to have a haircut in Zurich, how much in Germany, even though it means traveling to Germany. It does not seem to concern him that he goes to the place which caused him so much suffering. He does not seem to blame the younger generations of Germans. He often switches subjects, as if the fire he has come upon in memory will burn him and he must be spared for the moment until it overtakes him once more. He can be in the midst of describing the murder of his brother when he suddenly shifts to a detail he has told me about many times—how he went to Manon to have a cup of coffee, how he never eats all the food he has ordered but brings it home so he will have another meal of it later. Like Minnie in the nursing home in America whom I visit each week. At lunch, she drops part of the chicken covered with gravy into her large black leather purse. Never mind that whatever else is in the purse is now covered with thick gravy. But for Leiser, saving for later may have saved his life.

I know that Joseph should have returned home to America by now and that Leiser is waiting to hear from him, to see if what had happened, what he experienced was real, if Joseph will come back. I know that Leiser does not sleep in a regular bed. He keeps trying to tell me, *like in the army*, he says. *A sleeping bag?* I ask. He doesn't know what that means. We are talking through the veil of language—his German, Yiddish, Hebrew. My English, poor German, scant Yiddish and Hebrew. His difficulty with hearing in the first place. And when he is manic, his wish not to hear at all, but only to speak, to speak without stopping. Sometimes I have to hold the phone away from my ear. I feel so overwhelmed by his energy, his frenetic, powerful energy. I know that Ada has left hundreds of journals and that they are all over the floor. He tells me that if he cleans out the sleeping room and removes some sort of bed that she used, he will have a place for the journals. And he is trying to clear a place for Joseph, when and if Joseph returns. He doesn't forget to ask me if I am warm, if I have ordered oil. He doesn't remember that he's already asked me that many times and that I have answered him. I know that he is named the same name as my grandfather's father. I know that the name is repeated throughout the generations of our family. Eliezer.

Leiser is in the hospital having lost total vision in his left eye. The nurse saw him walking in the corridor during the night and gave him a sleeping tablet. *I told her that I should not be given sleeping medication. I can even kill somebody. I can do something very bad. I would even . . . once I went into the kitchen and turned everything . . . tore everything into pieces. I could kill even Ada.*

Now suddenly, Leiser sends what looks like a partial family tree but its conclusion tells where they were killed.

2

Frieda Rabinovitch: great-grandmother.
Heshel and Simche Damerecki-Rabinovitch: maternal grandparents.
Rubin and Esther Packer-Damerecki and their children, Meril, Leibka, Mendke Packer: sister of Leiser's mother.
Israel and Yentka Donski-Damerecki and their children, Sorela, Chanala, and two babies: sister of Leiser's mother.
Moshe Eliyahu and Chaye Libe Wolpe-Oppenheim: paternal grandparents.
Susmann and Esther Musikant-Wolpe and their children, Itke, Berele, Daniel Musikant: sister of Leiser's father Abraham.
Simon and Fruma Graz-Oppenheim and their daughter Sara Graz: Fruma, sister of Leiser's grandmother Chaye Libe Wolpe Oeppenheim.
Chaim Oppenheim, his wife Dora and their three children: Chaim, brother of Fruma Graz Oppenheim and Chaye Libe Wolpe Oppenheim.

Murdered in Keidan, Lithuania on August 28, 1941, in the pit dug on the banks of the Smilga stream.

Message from A. J. [a relative]: Leiser survived the German onslaught while hiding in a bunker. There was no particular evasive action on his behalf that secured his survival from the event. During the liquidation of the Kovno Ghetto (July 1944), all identified bunkers were bombed to the best of the Germans' ability. Those in the houses or caught fleeing from bunkers were murdered. Where Leiser was, there was a two-level bunker. He and his mother were in the upper level bunker and Rabbi Ephraim Oshry[3] and others in a bunker below. This lower bunker was well-constructed, and when the Germans bombed the top bunker, the bottom bunker remained concealed and intact.

Leiser and his mother survived the upper-level bunker explosion and were—with a luck Leiser doesn't understand—rounded up with other bunker survivors and taken to Waneustrasse, a collection point. There they were kept for a day or two before being loaded onto cattle cars and railed to Stutthof, Germany.

As for Rabbi Oshry, he and approximately eighteen others survived the liquidation explosions as well as the onslaught of the Germans and were liberated by the Russians in 1944 in Kaunas.

Leiser is in Sant' Agnese recuperating from surgery. He washes his socks and hangs them on the balcony outside his room to dry. He is told by the nurse that it is forbidden to do that. He asks: *What is this? Auschwitz?*

He looks out at Lago Maggiore and says: *All six million could fit into that lake.* On this day, he says, *it is the anniversary of the Kinder Aktion in the Kovno Ghetto.*[4] *The Germans made me collect the children to be murdered. They were put on a bus with windows darkened so no one could see in and the children couldn't see out. They were gassed on the bus. By the time they arrived at the Ninth Fort, nearly all were dead. They were thrown into pits there.* On this night he calls at 3 a.m., and again at 4 a.m., and an hour later, again.

Leiser has spent from eight in the morning until five in the evening at a printer's shop copying drawings of Ada's. All went well except for the drawing of Rabbi Kosofsky. *Rabbi Kosofsky was geshnippened, circumcised by the printer! From the left side and the right side. and the Rabbi can't take Ada to court!* The printer has taken away too much of the drawing. Leiser thinks better of this joke as he says it, as if to say that Ada is in the ground and it would be disrespectful.

Leiser took her last words on March 23, 2003, where she has written: "*Without Jews, the Christians would not have Jesus,*" and has attached them to the drawing of the circumcised Rabbi Kosofsky. It is for this that Ada might be taken before a jury, but she is nowhere to be found. Leiser wishes to tell the lady in the print shop: *"What you did to the rabbi, from the right and from the left, he would be very cross."*

We suddenly shift to Tessin, the house which he and Ada bought with some of the money she received for her paintings. It was her inspiring studio and Leiser gardened there. She often painted him in the garden. The house was a stable when they bought it—unlike the stables in the ghetto where he helped his mother to give birth. *I saw the lake and the mountains in the morning and the evening. You see the mountains and the snow.*

Now he speaks of the man who built a great synagogue in Jerusalem, a non-Jew. And about subscriptions he buys for others. And then the subject of sheitels, the marriage wigs worn by orthodox women. *They need five sheitels,* he says. *Each one costs close to three hundred francs.* The shifts are so rapid, I can barely keep up.

I come just now in. We spent the whole morning in the hospital. She had to stay there. They give her something in the vein. And then I brought her back. Timetable for her tablets. And then I left for the apothecary. Post office. She knows it. It is something unexpected. Ada felt already pain in her right side. Thought it was rheumatism. And she was given a massage. More pain. And it was like this—everything started in December. And at night Ada said the pain was moving around like in a tram station. This is not normal. After the X-ray she was sent to the emergency room. Since the chemotherapy she vomited only twice. Doctors are very nice. She made a drawing: Der Schmertz, the pain. It was very sad. Like Edvard Munch's "The Cry." She made it on paper, like she saw it before. The tree without leaves. I pass by it every day. The tree like a crucifixion. The tree that had the image of a devil in it. My interpretation: *She felt all of these things before. She didn't know what comes but she felt it. Everybody has cells but no one knows when they will wake up.*

Last night something happened to me. For the first time I heard Ada calling me. I got up. Did you ever have that happen? Did you hear of that?

I send Leiser information from a number of galleries and Holocaust museums about how to have Ada's paintings considered for their collections. For a Holocaust collection, the artist must have been in a concentration camp. He comments: *She was not in a concentration camp.*

For forty-four years, she was in a concentration camp with me. I cannot go back and change myself. Let them come and see for themselves. Did I show you my concentration camp number and the photograph in the ghetto with my star and documents from then? And the original war speech of Hitler? In Yad Vashem they sit there in an office like collection managers. They can do nothing for me. It is a pity. Even when one is sixty or sixty-two, one has to be in good health. When I was in America in nineteen eighty-one, perhaps then. Now, I am Basha the Blinder, Fishko the Lame from Keidan. I get only three hours' sleep. By me it is quarter to two in the morning. I think I will go to the police station. I need someone to talk to at two in the morning. You know we have open phones with a little table to put your things. Yesterday, I see a big red purse. No one is there. I open it, a whole collection of cards, but I don't look. I see cards, a passport and a lot of money. What am I going to do? I ask myself. I think of a finding place [lost and found]. *But when I come there the office is closed. It is a holiday for young men in Zurich. I take it to the police station. Now I am going the same way I came. I see a young woman. She is crying terribly. Are you the one who lost a wallet? But she couldn't speak German or English, only French and Portuguese. Come, I say, and I take her to the police station. The police had phoned a doctor in Portugal from the cards in her purse. They wanted to know if I took anything from the purse, but she looked and nothing was missing. She gave me an envelope and inside were a hundred Euros. I took the purse not to my own police station but to the center of Zurich. Now you go, I said to myself, the same way back. And that is how I found her. Sheherazade,* he tells me. As if he is Sheherazade, telling stories to stay alive. As if by telling stories he can prevent a calamity.

A thousand drawings and three thousand or more altogether. I have nobody to talk to. When will you go to sleep? Now I will have a glass of tea and sleep for a little. And then Stephen will come to the studio. I didn't want to shlep Ada's paintings hin and her. Her bouquet of paintings to the left and to the right [here he refers to the selections during the Holocaust]. *But I can't do it by myself. After I am gone, someone else will have to do it.*

Leiser wants to visit Dachau for the first time in fifty-eight years since his incarceration there. I am concerned that the visit there and his attempt to walk the miles of the forced march on which he was taken by the Germans might be too much for an elderly man. I remembered that he had been taken to St. Ottilien, a monastery, after his release. He was emaciated, ill with tuberculosis, and in need of care. I thought that if I contacted the fathers at St. Ottilien, it might soften the pain of going back to Dachau.

Leiser did go to St. Ottilien where he was kindly greeted by the fathers. On his return, he told me the following: *Dachau. Forced March to Bavaria—eight to ten days, thirty miles, no food or water. The Germans forced us into a pit. The pit was shaped like a bottle—the neck of the bottle was the route by which we entered the pit, the rest of the pit widened out like the body of the bottle. Likely the Germans would have killed us there, but the Americans arrived and a battle ensued. Some Germans fled, others were killed. Approximately half of those in the pit died of exhaustion and illness. Despite the fact that I had TB and was spitting up clots of blood, I saw something beautiful along the way, Waakirchen. We were the last group to leave Dachau in May nineteen forty-five. At St. Ottilien, when they took off the lice-ridden, filthy clothing, I asked that they save my number. I didn't know that my uncle David Wolpe was there. David was in a transport train from Dachau. He jumped from the train and hid in the forest and eventually came to St. Otillien near Bad Worishölen. I was locked on a certain floor, quarantined. Nuns looked after me there. David was in a part that was not quarantined. I asked why I couldn't go outside and I was told that I had TB. I didn't know what it was. I underwent pneumothorax.*

Two years after that first visit back to Dachau, Leiser talks of going again, this time with a German historian. We talk about St. Ottilien, the monastery where he stayed after liberation and which he visited after his first return to Dachau. *Yes*, he says, *St. Ottilien was one of the worst experiences of the war.* I was dumbfounded. I had thought that at last he and the others were comforted there, were cared for. Perhaps it is an American fantasy that once the doors of the concentration camps opened, the survivors—gravely ill, starving—were welcomed back into the world with care, that the horror was over. But it was nothing like that. Many who had managed to survive unimaginable horror could not survive what happened next. *I can't talk about it,* he says. *Read a certain book. It is called "Surviving the Americans."*[5] *You will find out everything you need to know.*

I located the book by Robert Hilliard and read it at once. The introduction begins this way: "'What's the difference between you Americans and the Nazis,' a concentration camp survivor said to me, a U.S. soldier in U.S.-occupied Germany a few months after World War II had ended in Europe, 'except that you don't have gas chambers!' The war was over and the survivors of the camps had been freed. But the Genocide that the Germans had begun did not end. . . . Genocide by neglect, some called it. Deliberate neglect, others suggested. . . . In the months following the end of the war, many of those who thought the defeat of the Nazis would release them from the living hell they had come to know under the German regime found themselves starved, raped and even shot by the same American forces that had freed them."

If ever there was testimony and witness to what each individual is capable of in righting the world, *Surviving the Americans* is such an example. Two young army privates—Robert Hilliard and Edward Herman—in the American occupation forces stationed near St. Ottilien found a way, by writing letters and secretly getting food into the monastery as well as medical supplies, to eventually claim the attention of President Truman and the American public about the horrendous conditions that survivors had to contend with. After some months, help began to arrive, and though many were lost, some including Leiser Wolpe and his uncle David Wolpe did manage to survive and to live their full span of life.

Did you know the men who killed your father and the others in the cellar of your apartment house on Laisvės Alėja? Two Lithuanians. Nazi sympathizers. I was the youngest in that cellar. I was the only survivor. Did you have any memories because of your visit to Dachau? I remember everything, like in a computer. Until I pass away. There was a village within eyesight of the concentration camp. They could see when we came and what was going on. But they couldn't help. They would be shot. Even if they wanted to help.

About other towns where Wolpe family members lived: *I was a child then. I went on a school trip to Vilnius and to Palanga, but not to Dotnuva, Josvainiai, not to Ariogala, Babtai, Girtigola, Ponevezh, Krak, Rasein, Shavl, Vilkomir, Utian, Vendzhigola, Yanova, Yosvine, Ruseiniai, Utian.*

The cellar—it was dark and full of blood.

On Ada's painting of Leiser attempting to help his father after he'd been shot in the cellar: *I don't yet understand her painting. The whole picture is like an X-ray, a shining light, like something white, a light that came from somewhere else. A light that covered me. I was the only one alive. A light from somewhere, a strange licht, as if from outer space. I don't understand Ada's painting. The artist doesn't always understand his own work. It comes from the unconscious. A light from God, a light from heaven, if you were a believer.*

When I ask Leiser how he and Ada first met, he says a German word I cannot make out. I ask him if he means in Yiddish *bashert*, fated. *No*, he says, his guardian angel helped him to meet her.

Don't go there alone, he tells me carefully. This is before I met him. But I know his voice. We talk on the phone quite often. He's given me a sacred task. But now he can't sleep at night, even his small share of sleep, thinking about it, about what I might uncover. But wasn't I the one who told him to stop going back to Dachau.

Don't go there alone. Take someone with you, he insists. Who does he think would be willing to go with me? To the cellar where all the men and boys who lived in his apartment house had been taken at four in the morning and shot. The place where his father died. Where he, only a boy himself, crawled out from among the dying men, wounded and bleeding, and climbed the steps to knock on the door of a family too frightened to open the door.

How many times have I walked past that very place—78 Laisvės Alėja, Freedom Way—in Kaunas. It is always the same. Not a word about what happened there. Like when I was in Keidan where he was born, at the Zhirgunai barns, and the others looked at one another knowingly. But they wouldn't say a word to me. Yet I knew something terrible had happened there. Just a stable. Where the horses were kept. Only later, reading a relative's account of the murders, is my sense of it confirmed. They were taken there, women and children, men, locked up with no food, no place to urinate or defecate, no place to sit or lie down and, after some days, taken to the massacre place in small groups, the young, healthy men first, then the women and children, murdered. Not all. Some were still alive when they were thrown into the pit. They tell that the earth heaved for days over that pit.

Reenacting the Holocaust: He is never in one place for long. In the apartment in Zurich, in the house in Tessin, in the atelier, in the basement, the attic, the flea market, on the tram. As if to create alternatives in the event of catastrophe.

He keeps possessions in all of these places, always packing and unpacking, moving items from place to place, carrying them up and down many flights of stairs. The atelier is not used at all for painting but is completely filled with boxes and items for the flea market. Only Leiser seems to know the pathways through the large space in order to get to Ada's paintings, which he brings out, one by one, as in a ceremony. One feels that he must not be disrupted in this ritual, nor helped, though many of the paintings are very large and heavy and boxes must be moved to get to them and he is elderly.

Ada's painting of Leiser holding his father who is shot in the cellar of 78 Laisvės Alėja. *Did it happen that way?* I ask him. *No. I was kneeling and when I held him, he was already dead.* He shows me his scar on his left arm and on his chest from the bullets. *In Dachau, we were awakened brutally every morning at four a.m.*

It is always with me. I cannot put it in a cupboard. It is good that you did not come in nineteen eighty-one. This is the right time. Ada's painting is a curtain between the Holocaust and me. They killed something in me. Without Ada I would not have lived. I ask why I did survive. Why did I not go to the Ninth Fort [the Czarist fortress where tens of thousands were killed] *with the others?*

I have brought to him a number of documents from the Kaunas archives which he doesn't seem to be able to concentrate on—a picture of his mother on an internal passport, a list of eligible voters with his family names, photographs of Laisvės Alėja. I tell him that 78 Laisvės Alėja is gone now and in its place a natural history museum. But I have taken pictures in the alley behind it which has some of the original buildings and even portions of the earlier buildings including the cellars. I have a picture of the pedestrian walkway, the post office, school, by which he might be able to identify the place where he had once lived. But he barely notices.

Though prior to my visit, he and Ada had asked that I record our conversations, once there he does not wish me to do so. The conversation is intensely painful, not because of its content but because of my feeling fixed at the point of a knife. News that I brought from a fellow survivor, Solly Ganor, author of *Light One Candle*,[6] that a group of Dachau survivors from Lithania meets every July at Dachau—since Leiser has returned to Dachau twice and hopes to do so again—does not seem to register for him.

At the airport. He stands there, a small, compact, solitary figure, wearing a cap, and waves to me. I turn around and he is still standing there. I wave again. And he waves. And I walk farther and turn and he is still standing there. I wave and walk away. I have the thought that he is like a small child who stands there and doesn't move from the spot and waves and waves until I am far out of sight. And I am filled with a terrible sadness.

Leiser worries about what will happen to Ada's paintings and to all the objects in his various domains after his death. *After all,* he says, *I am not Tutankhamen. I can't take anything with me.*

He calls again. He asks me how those survivors who stayed in Lithuania after the war can bear to pass each day by the places where their families were murdered. I have wondered the same thing. Usually they say they had no choice. They were not able to leave. Not to leave their families. Not enough money. Not under communism. No place to go.

He will tell me about Dr. Elkes (head of the Kaunas Ghetto Ältestenrat). But not on the phone. Only in person. About how Elkes tried to save Dr. Nabrisky in the ghetto. About how he could not. About how Elkes tried to stop the Aktion that took ten thousand of them to their deaths in one day. How Dr. Elkes was beaten and had to be carried back to the ghetto.

He will tell me about how his mother was pregnant and was due very soon to have her child, his small brother. How his own living brother was burned to death in the hospital—when the doctors and nurses and patients were locked inside and the hospital was set on fire. He did not understand why his brother was there in the first place. His mother gave birth, but after eight days the infant died. Two sons lost. He will tell me when I am there, with him, in the same room. But not on the phone.

How many times he circles these losses.

His wife Ada once made a painting of Leiser in the garden. He stands there among the tall flowers, among butterflies and birds. She paints him into the light. She leaves no shadow in her paintings that he might fall into. And when he is in her paintings, he does not dream about the killing.

In the end I do not know if I am a conduit for them. Or an imposter.

I don't wish even my enemies to be blind, Leiser begins. *I will tell you something very nice. I always like elephants. Because elephants—people think they are big monsters—they can think. They can talk. Not like human beings. To their keeper,* ein warter, *in German. He talks to the elephant and the elephant gets to know his voice. He knows he is not an elephant. You can teach him to say, "Thank you," and "Please," and now you have something and don't be afraid. You are not allowed to touch the body, only the ears and trunk and feet. Their skin is very sensitive and when you touch*

Leiser Wolpe, in the garden

them on the body they get afraid. Ada also loved the elephant because they brought flowers to the graves of dead elephants. Like a big matzevah, put flowers and grasses. And one day the elephant saw not breathing flowers but paper flowers. He didn't know they were paper. I was always interested in katzen and dogs, but mostly elephants. The keeper tells him to say "Thank you," and when the elephant is very happy, he takes his foot and stamps it and says, "Danke," and if he is very happy, he stamps his foot two times and says, "Danke, Danke," and if he is very very happy, he says "Danke Schoen," and then stamps his foot three times.

Now you have a phone call from a blind man. And he makes you laugh. I saw elephants in Africa. And in India they put us on the top of a big elephant and we went to the Taj Mahal. Ada would have a school holiday and she would say, "If you like you can come with me." So I went with her to China, to Bulgaria, to Yugoslavia, to Uzbekistan. Forty years ago. Ada was the youngest child. She wanted to study art with Diego Rivera in Mexico. She taught herself Spanish and went to the Mexican Consulate, but she couldn't get a visa because Africa was an apartheid country in those times. So she went to England in nineteen forty-eight.

Plungė. Massacre site. Jacob Bunke, artist

Ada's siblings were born in Plungė, Lithuania. Her brother, four years her senior, Lippy Lipschitz—her father wanted him to be a doctor. But he went to Paris to study to be a sculptor. When he was four years old in Plungė, they set out. It took them three months to make the journey to South Africa. Ada and I were married in the nineteen fifties. I met Lippy first and a friend of Ada's in London where she studied for ten years. Sometimes I think it would be better to be an elephant. He has a guardian, a shomer, a keeper. When the keeper says: You now stay here until I am back, and he will stay the whole night. If the keeper told him a lie, then the elephant would kill him. The elephant knows exactly when the keeper is sleeping. I could hear the shooting.

Leiser has abruptly changed the subject. The past has intruded without warning.

We are back in the Kovno Ghetto during the Great Aktion once again, where nearly ten thousand Jews are taken from the Ghetto to the Ninth Fort and killed over a period of forty-eight hours. *Nothing to do about it,* he goes on. I hurry to follow him. *Your book is like a mosaic, like weaving a carpet. You can make it a very good carpet or one with mistakes. It doesn't matter. To see what humans can do.* Now he switches to the fact that he is nearing his eightieth birthday. And he talks about how, in Switzerland, when a person turns eighty, they have a big celebration.

Each day I try to take hold of the fine thread that connected Leiser to me. I want to say this in the present tense—the thread that connects Leiser to me. Sometimes I imagine that I am holding one end of the thread and the other end is caught by the wind and is far away and there is no one holding the other end. Even for those who are near us, who live in this world with us, the thread of knowing them, knowing each other, can be broken. So I hold to Leiser's words as a living presence. What is this compelling power that drives us to need the connection to the past, our past? Through Leiser I am able to recover my own past, one that would have been invisible otherwise. Yet it is more than that. I think that through me Leiser was able to travel a little farther into the present. The gentle titration of movement—not holding too firmly, but holding on nonetheless while we are both in motion. The way Rilke says it in his poem "Herbst"—

Autumn

The leaves are falling, falling as from way off,
as though far gardens withered in the skies;
And in the nights the heavy earth is falling
from all the stars down into loneliness.
We all are falling. This hand falls.
And still there is one who holds this falling
endlessly gently in his hands.[7]

When I went into the sea, I saw a sea of blood. In Spain. I wanted to paint. I would paint only blood. Is something wrong with me? No. I was in Spain. In Palanga. In school. I was with the school in Palanga. An excursion. A few days. I was never to the seaside. Only Palanga. Then to Spain. I was so dirty. I have a feeling I have to wash myself three hundred times. It was not normal. In the first flat, no warm water, no shower, no real bed, a camping bed. First time I had a feeling, a sea of blood with dead people. Then it went away. Then I enjoyed it. A holiday in Spain and Italy. Mostly, I kept everything in order.

A blind man comes into the bank and asks for fifty thousand Swiss francs. The bank manager takes me into a room. I am old and blind, I tell him. And I can use the money.

Opened now a secret German archives after sixty-five years. Marchers from Dachau. Dead men walking. April twenty-ninth, nineteen forty-five. Dachau to Waakirchen. Star Paper from Johannesburg. Seventy-four dead marchers.

Though Leiser has told me parts of this memory a number of times, on this night he tells it in more detail. It is as if there are concentric circles around an inner core and he must start with the outermost circle which contains the barest details and with each telling he moves to an orbit closer to the fiery inner core of memory. For instance, this:

My mother and I are living in a stable for animals that adjoins a block house in Slobodka [Vilijampolė], Kovno Ghetto, after my father is murdered at Seventy-Eight Laisvės Alėja, with all the men and boys in the apartment house and all those up and down Laisvės Alėja. I was wounded but I crawled out of that basement to look for help. My younger brother

Chaim was burned alive in the hospital in Slobodka along with all the patients, doctors, and nurses. My mother is eight months pregnant and delivers a baby on the earthen floor of the stable whom she names Benjamin after the Biblical Joseph and his brothers, Benjamin the youngest son. Though I am sixteen, it is my duty to bury the placenta and a few days later when the infant dies, I, along with an older man, must bury the infant. My mother, Luba Damarecki Wolpe, ended up in Stutthof Concentration Camp.

Here is another telling of the infant brother's birth. New details are added. Does it mean that he can remember more with each subsequent telling? That part of the memory awakens another? And another? Or is it that he cannot bear to tell it whole? To put the whole image into his view at once? That he could be overwhelmed by doing so? Paul Russell, in *Trauma, Repetition & Affect Regulation*, speaks of repetition occurring "in lieu of something we cannot yet feel, a kind of affective incompetence" (4). The eventual goal—a gathering of the forces of earlier competence before the trauma occurred, in an effort toward emotional wholeness. But it was my sense that Leiser's use of repetition was as though to build an impermeable wall against what might burst through at any moment and take him under.

Or is there something else at work here? What is the nature of this continuous further elaboration? Repetition can sometimes bring the image before one sufficiently to confront it fully, to discover its truth or its meaning, to remove its potency. But here, somehow, the function seems different. It seems as if the repetition is a kind of infinite regress, that it might go on forever, like images in a mirror.

Nineteen forty-one. My mother was pregnant, eighth month. Stable. Earthen floor. One window. Clay hearth. My mother said to me: "Put on hot water. Call for Dr. Nabrisky." He came late in the evening. The baby was already born. The doctor gave me the placenta. "Put it into the earth." The baby lived only a few days. Came an elderly man, wrapped the baby in an old shirt. We took the infant to the Jewish cemetery and buried it.

Was it difficult for you?

Yes and no. I didn't understand all these things. My brother Chaim was burned in the hospital in Slobodka on October fourth, nineteen forty-one. Friday. The stable was where they cooked food for the pigs. It was attached to the only block house in the ghetto. It was made of moss and wood. Inside the block house lived other Jewish people.

October twenty-eighth: The Great Aktion. We were required to gather at Democrat Square. All would be killed who did not come. They were taken away to the Ninth Fort. The kleine ghetto, bridge. My mother and I were standing by the bridge to see what was happening in the small ghetto.

The block house next to the stable where we stayed had a cellar. When bad things happened, we went to the cellar. It had a small kitchen and fireplace. I could hide myself in the fireplace, behind the chimney in a small place behind a wall. When the Germans came, I could hide. My mother was a very interesting woman. The block house was on Majeo Gatvė? Or Marių Gatvė? It had one room, one bed. I could see it through a window. I am "The Blind Witness." I am eighty-two.

In nineteen forty-four I was sent from Stutthof to Dachau. We were liberated by the Ninth American Army. I spent one year in Germany and in nineteen forty-six went to Davos, Switzerland, to a TB sanatorium.

Last night I couldn't find Leiser. The sky was a soft dark velvet patch and it was empty. I seemed to be looking up. He had backed off, like God's angel that Rilke writes about who refuses to take the last breath of Moses, so that God himself must claim Moses's soul. Leiser is beyond me. Missing.

Aftermath: What we imagined was the opening of the metal gates and the revived souls rushing through into the air of spring, suddenly restored to the living, years of privation washed from their torn bodies, years of humiliation and torment and loss vanished in the light of freedom. But it was not to be. To get rid of the evidence, even the dead bodies were brought to the surface and arranged in stacks like firewood and set to burning. And for those few who had survived, some were taken on forced marches by the Nazis in a frantic attempt for their American liberators to find the death cages emptied. Most, already malnourished and weak, died along the way. Some were put on ships, starved for days and thrown into the sea, like my cousin whose sister drowned moments before reaching the shore. Of those who survived, some were taken to a monastery, or hospital, or left to fend for themselves. And some were kept in the very places where they had been imprisoned for so long under conditions not much better than before.

The tram driver suddenly caught sight of an elderly man with a white cane. He automatically pushed on the brake with all his might but nothing could halt the power of speed once attained; no inertia nor braking force was enough.

As Leiser fell into his new state of being, he was set aflame with the last of his energy, as his small brother had been set aflame in the locked hospital all those years ago. He knew at last what the boy had felt as he and his mother witnessed the burning, as his mother felt the first of her labor pains, as if at the moment of the death of twelve-year-old Chaim, Benjamin announced his wish to enter this world. That he too would last no more than a few days was beside the point.

The police did not mention what specifically had been Leiser's damage, thought by Stephen to be an act of kindness. But there was one more such act—a young mother who had sometimes stopped by to give Leiser his eye drops lest he not lose all sight in the remaining eye heard the police knocking on Leiser's door and went to learn what the commotion was all about.

Just as it was that Leiser, no longer himself, but with a heart that refused to stop beating, lay in a hospital bed for eight more hours.

When they told the young woman of the accident, she and a neighbor went to the hospital and stayed by Leiser's side until he took his last breath at exactly 1:15 in the morning—the time this sleepless man would likely have been in the kitchen preparing tea for the start of his long day.

3

On September 25, 2011, in the woods next to the massacre pit where twenty-nine of Leiser's family were murdered seventy-five years earlier, in the town of Kėdainiai (Keidan), Lithuania, I kept my promise to Leiser not to forget the names of our family. Rimantas Žirgulis, director of the Kėdainiai Regional Museum, worked for months to orchestrate a ceremony that included an artist's rendering of a steel wall with the engraved names of those who lay in the massacre pit. We lighted a menorah, and spoke of what happened in this place, and placed stones of remembrance. The children had embedded a golden menorah of flowers in the earth at the head of the burial place. A woman sang and two musicians—a drummer and trumpeter—opened and closed the ceremony. Leiser never dreamed that this remembrance would take place in the town of his birth.

Menorah made of flowers in Kėdainiai (Keidan). Drawings and paintings reproduced here are by the artist, Ada Lipschitz Wolpe

Chapter V

LIETŪKIS GARAGE MASSACRE

Sustok. Ir susimąstyk šižemė persunkta nekaltų žmonių krauju.
Be still. For the earth you walk on is filled with blood.

—Inscription on memorial at the
mass killing site, Alytus, Lithuania

On June 27, 1941, Jewish men were taken off the street in Kaunas, Lithuania, in broad daylight and brought to an automotive garage. They were first humiliated and then beaten to death. These acts were witnessed by many, some holding up small children to see.

Just as in the case of Leiser Wolpe, where over a nine-year period each contact and each telling of his experience brought him closer to the white heat at the core, so the multiple versions of witnesses to the Lietūkis Garage killings bring us not only closer to the events there but to the capacity of human beings to take in the immensity of what took place. They teach us how memory differs when it has carried that trauma as a living entity during the majority of one's life. It is of critical importance to understand how the internalization of these memories differs among perpetrators, collaborators, witnesses, survivors. And between parent and child made witness to this event. The memorial, a stone, sits in quiescence on the edge of a schoolyard, barely noticeable, and in no way does it convey the power and barbarity of what took place here in 1941.

What is the role of the bystander, what the nature of those who observe? Of what significance has this for our own response to injustice?

Daniel Bar-On makes a distinction between "bystander" and "witness"—bystander as behavior that is contextual, and situational as opposed to a personality syndrome. He provides examples of bystanders who might have helped to change the outcomes: the "opportunist" bystander chooses not to resist and revolt when he might have; the "simple person" who benefits from the Nazi regime, yet is willing to help Jews after the war; the "ideologically oriented" bystander, for example, the "physician who grew up with such racial hygiene theories and does not struggle to confront them"; the "career" bystander, academics and artists who "gave up [their] moral or ethical role for pragmatic reasons"; and the "institutionalized-rational-bystander" who "combines institutional vision with deep-rooted Christian anti-Semitism . . ." I think of a woman in Dotnuva, Lithuania, who told me that the priest in their village church told his congregation as they had witnessed the killing of all the Jews of this town that they "must not worry their hearts. That the Jews had killed Christ and this was their punishment." She told me that this brought no solace to her, nor did she believe his rationale. I was struck by her words and recognized the writings from the Gospel of John (14: 1–2): "Let not your heart be troubled. You believe in God; believe also in me. In my Father's house are many mansions. I go to prepare a place for you."

Bar-on also refers to the "professional bystander," who had a role in the "chemical process," for instance, who provided the gas Zyklon B for Auschwitz but was unconcerned about its use. Another was the architect who planned and executed technical facilities, crematoria. "Distant bystanders," far away but knowledgeable about the murders who lived in democratic countries, did little to save Jews. "Other-hating" bystanders, who lived in homogeneous villages witnessed the atrocities and did not act, and family members of perpetrators, "emotionally related bystanders," later saw themselves as "victims of the historical events." I know that each of us can point to situations in our own lives where as bystanders, in retrospect, we did not act promptly to change the outcome of a disturbing or dangerous situation.

What follows here are witness testimonies of a particular massacre that occurred at the very onset of the Nazi occupation of Lithuania. Would the outcome have been different had the large group of bystanders taken action against the killing?

The specificity of memory is notable in these memories, the powerful detail. And the discrepancies between them—the young man who climbed up on the bodies and played a harmonica, or an accordion, after beating the victims with a club. Some said that his parents had been exiled to Siberia and this was his retribution. Some focus on the use of water as a brutal instrument, others on the beatings. The affect of the person interviewed is quite different when speaking in the comfort of her home or at the actual site where these murders took place.

1

Vera Silkinaitė, age sixteen, has gone to the cemetery to tend her father's grave and encounters on the way a massacre taking place at the Lietūkis Garage in Kaunas, Lithuania. A group of Jewish men are dragged off the street and beaten to death in plain sight of other Lithuanians, some of whom hold up their children to see. The scene is filmed by the Germans.

> I thought that I had to take a ride to the cemetery and water the flowers . . . the cable car is not working any more. Then I turned down Žemaičių Street toward Donelaičio Street and to Vytautas Avenue. I saw people running and I thought—what happened there that everybody is running so fast? . . . They beat the poor people. They, the Jews, were already in a stupor because the scuffle started earlier—before I came. Some were badly beat up—I don't know if they were alive or not. But they did not move. They poured water on them with hoses. Then they came back to life. The others they continued to beat. And they beat them without any reason, absolutely none. . . . The only thing was there is the scuffle, and a slaughter. I can say for sure—slaughter. So some people, including me, did not stay there long. One of them I can still see, as he was lying on the ground, they poured water on him—but he never woke up. Another one started to move. He was next to the first one and had a gash there. Scar. And some staggered. So they beat them even more. And with sticks. They had sticks, rifle butts, and hoses. These were the main weapons. I did

not stay there too long because I got scared and ran to the cemetery. . . . The murderers. I don't know, maybe eight or nine of them. People looked and some of them right away turned and ran. But some stayed and said: "That's good, give it to the Jews, give it to the Jews." One, a child, was on the shoulders so he can see better. That I remember very well. And I thought, what kind of scene to show . . . they, the ones doing the beating cursed. Called them degenerates, stuffed animals, *žydpalaikis,* and all kinds of names. Only enthusiasts who stayed were very interested in this slaughter . . . they were laughing and screaming: "Beat the Jews, beat the Jews."[1]

2

This was told by Irena Čarževskienė, who witnessed the Lietūkis Garage killing. She was thirteen years old at the time.

Later, we started running toward the hospital, and maybe in the second block was Lietūkis's Garage. . . . Both of us are looking at the fence and suddenly we see that they are pouring water with a hose, with such a strong pressure in this person's mouth. And he is not able to swallow the water so fast. The water is going down by itself and suddenly it is growing right here. His stomach is blowing up. Another one came up and with a crowbar hit him in the stomach, and suddenly through the hole in the stomach the intestines started coming out. And the intestines fell out right here. And they cleaned up the blood with the same hose, and the blood was running on the roadway. It was so horrible, you know, to watch, because I saw that the first time in my life. And the person, you understand. . . . From that I decided he was not tied up, because he used to fall down and then they again revived him with the hose. He was still moving, still alive. On one word, they tortured the man very bad. Now the doctors don't let me. . . . It would be understandable if an animal was tortured and die in such suffering. . . . And so they fell out. . . . That's all I saw. All my attention was pointed to the way he was tortured. So I cannot tell the nationality, because all I saw was the blood. . . . And also I remember very well that a plane came from the front, here along the avenue, and the plane was not a military, but I don't know what kind, maybe sports plane, or maybe like we had before the *kukurūznikas*. The pilot . . . he was flying so low that I saw he had a leather jacket. And it was very clear that he was taking pictures. He was flying by himself. We saw his face and he was holding something close to his face. He was taking pictures, or making a film. And the plane was flying above the garage.[2]

3

This partial interview was told by Jasiūnas Rimgaudas, who was ten years old at the time he witnessed this. Later in the interview he says that the man who came to arrest his father was a Jew and that his family had hidden a Jewish girl when her mother went to forced labor.

O, in the garage. . . . You know in the garage, that was when we the children. . . . We were getting into every place. Where other people were robbing the stores, taking out stuff. And I somehow got mixed up in that. . . . I saw, you see, how in the garage a group of people, you see—the nationality I can't tell—and who they were, Jews or no. . . . So that's how . . . you see, they were taking garbage from one corner to another with cupped hands. In the middle they were hit with a whip. And another one was pouring water, you see, on them. When the garbage is taken to one corner, then they were told to take garbage from the other corner and . . . and then again. And again, when they were running they were beaten with a whip and then water was poured on them again. I was not standing there too long. I didn't watch. I thought it was so cruel. And I left. I went to my grandmother in Sanciai. After about four or five hours I came back, also after this event I thought I'd see what happened. And there was a pile of dead bodies. They were already killed. How they were killed I didn't see. But it was a pile of corpses. And they were dancing in a circle, playing on an accordion, they were drunk. That's how it ended. And later where they were taken, that I don't know. Where they were buried?[3]

4

From the manuscript of Dimitri Gelpernas's *Kovno Ghetto Diary*:

Other Jews were forced to gather one afternoon in the courtyard of a garage at 43 Vytautas Avenue (now Lenin Prospect), in the centre of the city. Some of them were killed with shovels, iron bars, or by other barbaric methods. Bodies were thrown into a pile. One of the executioners climbed on top of this pile and began playing harmonica. The others, drunk on vodka and at the sight of human blood, sang with him and danced. Among those rushed to witness the terrifying event were German officers with cameras in their hands. The fascists were in a hurry to photograph the harrowing scene.

All those events showed the true face of fascism and deeply angered the whole city. Lithuanian doctors Kutergienė, Staugaitis, Alekna, Kairiūkštis, woman writer Bortkiavičiene and others tried to persuade the invaders to stop Jewish pogroms. German leaders warned them against interference in this matter; if they showed compassion for Jews, they would finish up sharing their fate.[4]

5

This account was told by Dr. Max Solc, brother-in-law of William Mishell, author of *Kaddish for Kovno: Life and Death in a Lithuanian Ghetto 1941–1945*.

You know the Lietūkis garage across from our clinic. I just saw a massacre of Jews which is beyond description. A group of Jews were brought in from the street and forced to clean the garage floor of horse manure with their bare hands. These Jews were treated very harshly. A whole group of civilians stood outside the garage and were observing the spectacle. When the men completed their work, they were led to the water hoses and, apparently, instructed to wash up. Suddenly, a group of partisans decided to have some fun and a massacre began. With spades, sticks, rifle butts, crowbars, and other tools from the garage they started assaulting the Jews. There must have been at least fifty or more Jews, all of them severely wounded, lying on the pavement crying and moaning. The partisans then grabbed many Jews by their hair and dragged them across the lot to the amusement of the bystanders. When the Jews collapsed, they turned the hoses on them and revived them. Once revived, they again beat them until they died. Then, later, another group of Jews was brought in to wash up the pavement and to remove the bodies.[5]

6

Report of an Oberst:

> I received orders to travel to Sixteenth Army Headquarters which was stationed in Kovno, and arrange quarters for the staff of the army group liaising with them. I arrived on the morning of 27 June. While I was traveling through the town I went past a petrol station that was surrounded by a dense crowd of people. There was a large number of women in the crowd and they had lifted up their children or stood them on chairs or boxes so that they could see better. At first I thought this must be a victory celebration or some type of sporting event because of the cheering, clapping and laughter that kept breaking out. However, when I inquired what was happening I was told that the Death-dealer of Kovno was at work and that this was where collaborators and traitors were finally meted out their rightful punishment! When I stepped closer, however, I became witness to probably the most frightful event that I had seen during the course of two world wars.

On the concrete forecourt of the petrol station a blond man of medium height, aged about twenty-five, stood leaning on a wooden club, resting. The club was as thick as his arm and came up to his chest. At his feet lay about fifteen to twenty dead or dying people. Water flowed continuously from a hose washing blood away into the drainage gully. Just a few steps behind this man some twenty men, guarded by armed civilians, stood waiting for their cruel execution in silent submission. In response to a cursory wave, the next man stepped forward silently and was then beaten to death with the wooden club in the most bestial manner, each blow accompanied by enthusiastic shouts from the audience.

At the staff office I subsequently learned that other people already knew about these mass executions, and that they had naturally aroused in them the same feelings of horror and outrage as they had in me. It was, however, explained to me that they were apparently a *spontaneous action* on the part of the Lithuanian population in retaliation against the collaborators and traitors of the recently ended Russian occupation. Consequently, these cruel excesses had to be viewed as purely internal conflicts which the Lithuanian state itself had to deal with, that is, without the intervention of the German army. Orders to this effect had been received "from above." I was also told that the public executions had already been forbidden and it was hoped that this prohibition order would be sufficient to restore calm and order.

7

From the testimony of a German photographer:

There were no more significant clashes in the city. Close to my quarters I noticed a crowd of people in the forecourt of a petrol station which was surrounded by a wall on three sides. The way to the road was completely blocked by a wall of people. I was confronted by the following scene: In the left corner of the yard there was a group of men aged between thirty and fifty. There must have been forty to fifty of them. They were herded together and kept under guard by some civilians. The civilians were armed with rifles and wore armbands, as can be seen in the picture I took. A young man—he must have been Lithuanian—with rolled-up sleeves was armed with an iron crowbar. He dragged out one man at a time from the group and struck him with the crowbar with one or more blows in the back of his head. Within three-quarters of an hour he had beaten to death the entire group of forty-five to fifty people in this way. I took a series of photographs of the victims. After the entire group had been beaten to death, the young man put the crowbar to one side, fetched an accordion and went and stood on the mountain of corpses and played the Lithuanian national anthem. I recognized the tune and was informed by bystanders that this was the national anthem. The behavior of the civilians present (women and children) was unbelievable. After each man had been killed they began to clap and when the national anthem started up they joined in singing and clapping. In the front row there were women with small children in their arms who stayed there right until the end of the whole proceedings.

Part Two

Chapter VI

Return

Witness, Survivor, Next Generation

1

As we hover over the airport in Vilnius, Lithuania, I see below a landing area filled with antique planes, remnants from earlier wars and occupations, mingled with horse-drawn carts, the kind used to carry bales of hay, the staves of each wagon sloping toward the center. A cart like the one my friend Yocheved—buried under a mound of hay—rode when she escaped from the Kovno Ghetto to begin her journey to freedom on a freezing January night. Carts like the ones my Lithuanian grandfather pulled in West Virginia when he escaped a twenty-five-year conscription into the Czar's army. It was as if one century has crossed the axis of another.

2

Though sleep had eluded me for several days, I walked out on the streets of Vilnius as though I had always been there. It felt as familiar to me as my childhood home in America. I seemed to know the way across the river, the way back to the Jewish quarter. My feet knew the way. And I recognized the tiny pears my mother loved, like the ones we call Seckel pears, ripening on the trees overhead. I took a tram after a while, but I couldn't figure out how to pay the driver who was shielded by a glass partition. He shrugged. I got off. I walked all that afternoon in a country whose streets seemed utterly familiar to me. It was cold that late summer. Women wore woolen scarves and heavy sweaters. Men wore jackets. This was the land of the midnight sun. You could walk safely until late at night, and though it grew dark then, it never grew entirely dark. By 4:30 in the morning, the sun was beginning to rise.

I didn't yet know the language. Lithuanian, an extraordinarily ancient language whose closest relative is Sanskrit, is not part of the contemporary polyglot vernacular many of us are acquainted with—our bit of French or Italian or German or Spanish. Curious, even though America is filled with numerous languages and dialects from Ethiopia to Kenya to Iraq. Lithuanian—a beautiful, haunting Indo-European language that becomes part of one's consciousness after a few days in Lithuania.

Language: Litvak Yiddish, the beautiful Yiddish of my childhood. My father's first language, my grandmother's tongue. The secret language of my parents. Across the hiatus of a lifetime, the language of Yiddish stretched its welcoming bridge of sound. In some towns in Lithuania, there were once so many Jewish people that the Lithuanian non-Jews spoke Yiddish as well. In order for the Jews not to be understood, they spoke Hebrew. In towns like Dotnuva, where so many of my family had once lived.

3

My various attempts to locate a guide failed. My Lithuanian language skills were, at that time, nonexistent. Suddenly the hotel phone rang. A young woman announced that she was interested in my search and would like to be my guide. To this day, neither of us knows how this happened.

How did Regina Kopilevich know that I wanted to explore the many towns and villages of my forebears? How did she know where I was staying? And how was it that the first place she took me was to a town called Kėdainiai (Keidan) where members of my family had lived for centuries, and where twenty-nine that we know of were killed in

August 1941 in the massacre pit there. Or that many years later, in 2011, I would stand in that place to honor and remember some two thousand and seventy-six who lay in that pit. That Rimantas Žirgulis, a remarkable young man who was director of the museum there and was preserving Jewish memories and artifacts, had arranged with an artist to create a metal wall upon which the names of those buried were engraved.

Regina Kopilevich

Yudel Ronder

And Regina Kopilevich had arranged for a survivor of Kėdainiai to walk with us, telling us about each Jewish family who had once lived there. I did not know then that the Krost house on Gedimino Gatvė belonged once to the family whose daughter Masha Krost was to become my close friend here in America, by now the matriarch of the Mervis family. Nor that my cousin and uncle, Leiser Wolpe and David Wolpe, the latter a well-known writer/poet who ended up in South Africa, were raised here. Leiser and David survived the Kovno Ghetto and Dachau Concentration Camp. I had no idea that Leiser Wolpe was alive, that we would become friends, that we would speak to each other daily for nine years. Nor that David Wolpe was alive. I did not know that my guide in Kėdainiai would be Yudel Ronder, my friend until his death. That even when he could no longer speak, we still visited and that I relished his company and was grateful to have known him.

The haunting images of those who become key figures in our lives have a way of rising to the surface out of all the images that live within us, in my case for some eighty years. I had thought at first to create categories, to put these souls into proper boxes, to make things clear. But it seems to do more justice to them to permit them to appear as I go along. "Here," says Yudel Ronder, pointing to a small wooden house in Kėdainiai, "is where the wet nurse lived who sustained me when my mother wasn't able to." "And here," he says, pointing to another house, "is where the great thinker and scholar Moshe-Leib Lilienblum was born, one of the forerunners of Zionism. And here is where a six-year-old boy from Vilna came to study. He was later known as the Gaon of Vilna."

4

On that same day we drove to Dotnuva, the home of many of our Wolpes. As we passed by those selling produce, an elderly woman ran down the dusty road after our car and began to weep and call out. We took her into the car; she sat beside me and told the story of the Jews of Dotnuva, how they were taken to a pit and murdered. How one

Produce stand in Dotnuva

survived, a man who came back to his house which he had entrusted to his neighbors. By the miracle of his survival, he was not so lucky the second time. His neighbors turned him in and he died a second time. Why does this woman tell such a story to perfect strangers?

July 1994: I decide to return to Dotnuva this summer, the town where Jankel (Jacob) Volpe, the father of my mother's cousin Masha Wolpe, was born. The town where my mother's cousins Rena, Leah, and Shimon Lopaiko were born and raised. I decide to try to find the woman who had run after our car the previous summer, to learn more about why she had done so and to see if she might remember my family.

But it was more than all of that. The town haunted me. For a year I had thought about the faces of those who were selling their produce

Aleksandra Balandienė and her husband

out of doors as we entered the town, the metal scale whose pans held cucumbers and apples, an aluminum pot full of mushrooms which looked exactly like the pot I still have from my grandmother that she used to make gefilte fish for Passover, the tall enamel container with a metal and wooden handle exactly like the one my mother gave me that belonged to my grandmother, this one filled with berries. I thought of each face, faces without joy, faces that had endured hardship. I wanted to know about them.

Regina arranged a visit with Aleksandra (Ola) Balandienė in Dotnuva. We found Mrs. Balandienė and her husband, found her at home on July 20—a beautiful, well-kept home with a wonderful flourishing garden full of daisies, vegetables, birch trees. Entering her house, removing our shoes, we are taken to the living room through the kitchen where cheese is being made and a large bowl full of butter. Her son and daughter-in-law are also there. We talk a while, in various languages, mostly with Regina's immense fluency in all of them.

Regina Kopilevich, daughter-in-law and son of Aleksandra Balandienė, seated, Rachel Langosch (author's granddaughter)

Ola Balandienė, as if she had been questioned about the ownership of her house—formerly a Jew's house—quietly went to fetch a tattered brown paper portfolio, like one issued from a lawyer's office. I thought it might contain photographs or documents from the war years, or birth certificates. But as she carefully untied the laces that bound it and brought out the documents, I realized these had to do with the sale and ownership of her house, that she was making sure we understood that her house had not been appropriated from the Jews illegally but that it had been, in fact, bought quite legally from its Jewish owners—an issue that had not crossed my mind.

But she seemed determined to make this clear. She explained that when the Jewish owner, Sara Levinsteinaitė, returned from Russian exile to search for those properties and possessions that had belonged to her mother, she said that she could not wash her hands in the blood of her mother. "If you do not buy this house, I will put it on fire," she told Ola Balandienė. So they bought the house and the cattle. They invited her—this was in 1946—to return.

"When I go to bed, I remember all the beds of their children—there were seven in the family. I remember one of the girls, Sara, daughter of Yudel, when she was to be brought to her death, she came back to say goodbye to me," Ola tells me. Then Mrs. Balandienė turned toward me and searched my face for a long moment. "You look like someone I knew many years ago." My heart quickened. "Like Leah. Leah Lopaiko," she said. My mother's cousin.

I could not believe my ears. Leah, her brother Shimon with a red birthmark, and Rena, their sister, whom I had known and loved, who had died at the end of a very long and good life here in Washington. I would never have thought to ask about that particular branch of the family. People in America had assured me that the name didn't sound like a Jewish Lithuanian name, and no one seemed to know exactly where this part of the family had come from in Lithuania. I was looking for Wolpe or Volpe or Wolpa or Volpaitė, Volpienė. Leah hid during the war and lived in Lithuania after the war. Her parents were killed during the war years. Lopaiko had a small shop, sold sugar and other foodstuffs. Leah had been Mrs. Balandienė's childhood friend. She was six years her senior. "The mother was tall," Mrs. Balandienė said. Like all our Wolpe women, I thought.

"Many non-Jewish people in Dotnuva understood Yiddish," she told me. "When the Jewish people in the town wanted to speak so they would not be understood, they spoke in Hebrew." I notice a family portrait on the wall—a mother, father, and a small son. "We lost a son in 1942 of influenza. There was no medicine then, nothing to do to help him," she told me.

5

I wanted to know why Mrs. Balandienė had run after us last summer, why she had shared her horrific memory of the Jewish man who had escaped from the massacre pit only to be turned in and killed. "Zundel Kagan," she told me.

> His family owned a large manufacturing company. Before he was brought to the pit in Krakės, he left his property to another rich family. When he escaped from the pit and came back to Dotnuva with an eighteen-year-old boy from Krakės [here she uses the Litvak pronunciation], to find those to whom they had left all their goods, someone went to the Germans, informed on Kagan and turned him in. If the Kagan family had given their property to a poor family, they would have helped him. It would have been easy for such a family to hide him. There was a huge amount of land, easy to hide them. They were held in a house in Dotnuva and killed near the Jewish cemetery by Lithuanians from Kaunas. After the war, the killer served for twenty-five years. He was found by a resident of Dotnuva, a man who worked for the NKVD and went to Kaunas and found him in the cinema—Joncavičius. This was unusual because most, if they served any time at all for their crimes against humanity, were not charged in this way but for other minor infractions with either no prison terms or very brief ones.

A year later, Aleksandra talked about how it was to spend Passover with my family, how it was to celebrate Simchas Torah with them. She is the key to my past. As is Josvainiai where I have gone to take a picture for the poet Stanley Kunitz—for this was the birthplace of his mother who bore the same family name as mine, Volpe. I discover a Volpe gravestone bearing the name repeated from generation to generation—Eliahu Akiba. The same name as my maternal grandmother's father. Gravestones tell us a great deal.

6

I went back to Dotnuva on each return trip to visit Aleksandra. It is curious about language. Aleksandra spoke Polish, Russian, Lithuanian, German, and some Yiddish. Yet so much of our communication was done without words.

"Our Father," Aleksandra said when she spoke of her husband, with such respect. But one year on my return to her, her head is covered with a black scarf. I am always afraid that she will be gone, that her life will be over and I will not find her anymore in this tiny village. And then my link through her will become invisible. Like the objects of my mother that seemed to relinquish their life once she was no longer alive. As long as Aleksandra is alive, so do my cousins live in Dotnuva. As long as she can tell stories about them.

Her husband has died. We cannot console her this time: she speaks of her longing to go and lie down in the graveyard next to him. She can see his grave from her window. I remember that she sings in her church at weddings and funerals and ask if she will sing something. She goes to find her Bible and begins. For months afterward, I hold my tape recorder to my ear and I sing with her: "Marija, Marija." I only find out now, on this day of America's Independence, that when the Lithuanians were hauled off to Siberia by the hundreds and thousands, they sang this beautiful, sad song. It begins this way:

> Marija! Marija!
> Skaisčiausia lelija!
> Tu švieti aukštai ant Dangaus!

Palengvink vergiją!
Išgelbėk nuo priešo baisaus!
Mes, klystantys žmonės,
Maldaujam malonės;
Mary, Mary,
You luminous lily,
You shine in the heavens on high.
Alleviate servitude
Assist humanity
Save us from terrible foes.

7

It is strange how the arrow keeps pointing to Dotnuva. Over the years in America we had been collecting family history information and photographs that we hoped would eventually result in a family gathering. We thought we might end up with forty names or so; we actually had

Masha Wolpe and Family

nine hundred by the time we did gather the remaining members of the family together in 1998 in Washington, D.C. Family came from South Africa, Australia, Israel, England, and throughout the United States.

In the process of this work, I learn the details of my cousin's survival. Masha Wolpe Baras, born in Kaunas, Lithuania, survived the Kovno Ghetto, prison, and Stutthof Concentration Camp. At the time of liberation, after a forced march, she was put on a German ship without food or water for eight days and was then thrown into the sea. Her sister Pearl, the last survivor of her immediate family, drowned moments before reaching shore. Masha swam to Kiel, Germany. She lay in the surf, half conscious, and was discovered by a British soldier. When he realized she was still alive, he carried her to a nearby hospital.

Now years later she tells about her part of our family:

> My father Jacob Wolpe; my mother Sheine Solsky Wolpe (born in Josvainiai); my brother Elisha Wolpe; my sister Pearl Wolpe. My father and all his brothers and sisters were born in a small town in Lithuania named Dotnuva. Dotnuva was a Wolpe town. Our grandfather, Eliahu Akiba Wolpe, owned the whole town until the First World War. He was in the lumber business and owned and sold forests. My father started a flax processing business after the First World War. He owned two factories in Šiauliai, Lithuania and one in Latvia. My father died in Dachau Concentration Camp with my brother Elisha. My mother died in Stutthof Concentration Camp.
>
> My father had two brothers in Kovno, Abraham and Heshel, both burned to death in Ghetto Kovno; one sister, Feiga Masha Lopaiko, killed in Dotnuva, One brother, Julius Wolpe, to avoid a twenty-five-year conscription in the Czar's Army came to America in 1904. Many aunts and cousins were killed.[1]

Masha was in Italy in an internment camp when a U.S. Army captain questioned her about any relatives in America who might help her. She had never met Julius, her father's brother, who had left Dotnuva before she was born. The captain offered to place an ad in a New York newspaper for Julius Wolpe and his niece, Masha, who had somehow managed to survive. This was well before the digital age. Yet the ad came to the attention of her uncle Julius Wolpe who immediately sent a cable to her: "Please come to America. Be well. Have courage. We love you. Uncle Julius." The next day he sent the following message: "Please advise me your need. Will do everything possible to help. With love, Julius Wolpe, 3322 14th Street, N.W., Washington, D.C."

There was a quota system in the U.S. Despite the assistance of the Joint Distribution Committee and HIAS, the Hebrew Immigrant Aid Society, and family members, it took another four years before Masha Wolpe was able to come to the United States.

8

When Masha was a teenager in the Kovno Ghetto, the Jewish partisans came to ask her mother if she could serve as a messenger for them. Her mother stated that the girl was a child. "That's what we want," they told her. Masha wanted to help. She was made to memorize letters and numbers, which were then conveyed to those in the forest and interpreted. This way, if she was discovered, she would not have tangible information. She describes being afraid of the huge trees in the forest. At one point she and the partisans were surrounded by Germans, forced to dig a pit, and lined up in front of the pit. Then the Germans stood behind them shooting everyone. But they shot over Masha's head. She lay without moving from the place where she had fallen until dark. The shooters went off to drink and celebrate. That night Masha returned to the Ghetto.

She claimed that she and her family knew what was in store for them even at the time when they were forced into the ghetto in August 1941. Her family was wealthy. They had a car and a chauffeur. Her mother bought her clothing in Paris. Her father did business all over Europe. She believed that she would not survive the war, but when she was in prison, the non-Jewish women there told her not to waste her tears, that she was to be executed in the morning. She rose up and announced that not only would she live, but she would live to teach Jewish children Hebrew. And so she did, first as the founding teacher of the Charles E. Smith Jewish Day School in Washington, D.C., later in Michigan, and again in Washington once more.

In Italy after the war, as she waited for passage to America, she completed four years of college and went to the Sorbonne as well. Masha Wolpe spoke of not wanting to block any of her memories because then she would not be close to her family.

A few words here about humor: Masha's daughter Sheila and I are talking about our problems with doctors. Masha is quietly listening in the background. When we are done, she announces that she doesn't go to doctors, "*Gotts a dankin*" (Thank God!). We call this the "Masha Wolpe theory of medical intervention!"

Today on the drive home from the Survivor's Gathering at the tenth anniversary of the United States Holocaust Memorial Museum, she says to her daughter who is unsure of the way, "Just keep driving! You'll get somewhere!"

Just before the seating for the Elie Wiesel talk at the museum, a woman is deliberating out loud about which seat to take. She tries out first one row and then another, one seat and another. "It's not such a big decision," Masha says in a loud voice. The woman does not take it kindly. In that context, it was ironic—where people had gone through such terrible experiences, decisions that cost their lives, the search for the right seat seemed trivial. Yet it surfaced like an unconscious remnant of earlier decisions in the Ghetto or concentration camp whose outcome might determine survival and over which people had little or no control.

Masha describes a "mistake" she made. She was going out to forced labor at Aleksotas at the airport one day. She was sick and escaped from the brigade and walked to Laisvės Alėja to a pharmacy to get some medicine. As she was ordering the medicine, two Gestapo members walked in. Whether it was because of her nervousness or something else, they realized she was a Jew and began to chase her. She ran into a church on Laisvės Alėja and stood in line with those waiting to receive communion. When it was her turn, she whispered to the priest that two Germans were behind her in the church and would harm her. The priest took her into the confessional and allowed her to escape through the back door of the church. To this day she doesn't know what happened to the priest. Nor who he was.

Masha has requested that her video interview with the Shoah Foundation not be viewed by family members until after her death. When cousin Don Wolpe protests that he will never see it because he will be gone before she is, she laughs. And when I say that I won't be able to ask her questions based on her interview, she says that I can ask her any questions I have. I know she means this. For weeks before this interview, she told me that she took to eating the dark, Lithuanian bread. Later, when we went to war with Iraq again, she took to eating the dark bread, like the small rations that could not appease the terrible hunger during the Holocaust.

Today was a hard day for Masha at the gathering of survivors. She seemed to find little consolation in meeting those whom she had known sixty years before. In the days before her death on September 18, 2015, we sang Yiddish songs together, such as "Oyfn Pripetchik," about a rabbi teaching his young students the *alef bet,* and later, in the song a lament about exile and how the words will provide strength. And earlier, on her birthday, we share a poem by Jacob Glatstein:

> I love my sad God,
> my brother refugee.
> I love to sit down
> on a stone with him and
> tell him everything.
> Here he sits, my friend,
> his arm around me, sharing
> my last crumb . . . now my God sleeps
> while I keep watch.

9

Over the years I have been struck by a continuing conversation regarding the fear of Lithuanians to speak about what they witnessed. In the villages we visited, it has not been my experience that this was so, but perhaps I did not represent any kind of a threat to those with whom I talked. I did not represent any official position; I lived very far away and was not reporting to a press office or government agency. I would not be talking to any official office within Lithuania. People seemed relieved to talk after years of fear and silence, to give voice to what they had experienced. And the light of a camera was not shining in their eyes. And with me were those like Regina Kopilevich who understood very well what they had gone through and knew the various languages through which their experiences were filtered and knew how to gently open the door to their trust. And we respected that trust.

10

Now my granddaughter, Rachel Langosch, speaks. It is 2002 and she is nineteen years old. What are her first impressions as she begins her journey with me to Lithuania?

> I was always fascinated with my grandmother's mysterious annual journeys to Vilnius, Lithuania, and her fascination with a community of people that none of my immediate family members knew much about. She would often come home with photographs and documents from her travels as well as the history of our family. She had collected the narratives of living relatives who once knew Lithuania in the post–World War II years. It was the mysterious appeal of such a faraway place, a place that held so much historical information through both the spoken accounts as well as landscape. This is what led to my own personal interest and decision to travel to Lithuania with my grandmother, Myra Sklarew.[2]

She goes on to explore the political aims imposed upon Lithuanians by communist control in the postwar years and how these affected the silencing of memory regarding the Holocaust and the effort by the remnant of Jewish survivors to preserve and document their history.

It was Rachel's initial entry to Vilnius, Lithuania, and her expectations of what she would find that were so dissonant with what she actually witnessed.

Rachel Langosch

To my surprise, I found myself immersed within a cosmopolitan city overwhelmed by numerous Internet cafes, restaurants, and large storefront advertisements of Jennifer Lopez promoting her latest perfumes. . . . My grandmother's stories often reflected intimate sharing of personal histories in small village homes. The world of modern elements seemed to hold no place for the memory of its past. Why had this culture transformed so abruptly and consciously to bury the horrors of the past? Where did the memories of Holocaust survivors and others affected by the drastic political and social changes of the past fit into this chic cosmopolitan present-day society? What are the cultural factors that led to the silencing of the memories of Lithuania's Jewish past? And more importantly what present-day factors have allowed for the apparent emergence of Holocaust studies primarily in Lithuania through literary, filmic and other culturally collective elements in the past decade?

> Although my great-grandmother left Lithuania before the start of WWII, many other members of our family were directly affected by the destruction and power inflicted upon the Lithuanians during the war.[3]

Rachel Langosch was confronted by an urgency she witnessed at Lithuanian lectures and with archivists for her generation to remember and rekindle learning about the Holocaust. She speaks of the desire of the young to focus upon the present and future. In her correspondence with survivor Solly Ganor (*Light One Candle*, 1995), he writes:

> The second generation survivors have a hard time in coping with their parents' Holocaust experiences. Many of the survivors avoid telling their offspring the horrors, because they wish to spare them the mental anguish. I am lately getting many e-mails from second-generation survivors whose parents have died. Now that they are gone, they have realized that they missed the opportunity to speak to their parents about their experiences. Many of them are in real distress about it and consult me about what to do. I try to answer their questions as much as I can.[4]

Rachel Langosch concludes that

> if I had merely traveled to Lithuania and stayed in the apartment on the bustling Stiklių Street filled with cafes and small shops, I may have never realized that I was actually living in the former Jewish ghetto and walking on the cobblestones that my ancestors walked on only sixty years prior with Jewish armbands and sunset curfews. There was no evidence of this history to the naïve visitor, which greatly disturbed me. It was only the "rememory" of the streets of the old Lithuanian ghetto that I walked down with a Holocaust survivor, who shared her memories with me, that the pictures of this history could take shape for myself. . . . The past social and political intentions to actively forget the Holocaust's existence have triggered the urgent and vital responses from the Jewish Lithuanian community to document and preserve these same memories.[5]

I would add only that other members of the community, as we shall see in the case of Rimantas Žirgulis and others, have done much to bring this history into the light.

Chapter VII

Trauma Made Manifest

Its Persistent Forms

1. The Erasure of Language: Lithuanian language vanished though all other languages are retained.

2. The Alteration of a Familiar Landscape: The first visit to the sea after the Holocaust—the sea waters have turned to blood.

3. Symbolic Condensation: A diagonal line represents the emptying of the Kovno Ghetto as some 9,200 inhabitants are made to walk up a diagonal hill to the Ninth Fort where they will be killed.

1

Though trauma can take many forms, three that are explored here had their origins during the German occupation of Lithuania from 1941–44—the erasure of language, the alteration of a familiar landscape, and symbolic condensation.

For a number of people who were fluent in Lithuanian and knew many other languages, Lithuanian seemed to vanish, though all other languages are retained. In terms of the alteration of a familiar landscape, one survivor describes his first visit to the sea after Liberation. The sea waters appear to have turned to blood. Many have described how a condensed image can evoke a major Aktion: a diagonal line in a painting brings the survivor not only to the memory of 9,200 being marched up a diagonal hill to their deaths, but also to the experience of being back there at the present moment.

2

Sam Schalkowsky never lost the ability to speak and understand all the many languages he knew, only Lithuanian, a language he had once spoken with ease. "I have been puzzled by the fact that of all the languages that I knew before the war, only Lithuanian was—selectively and completely—wiped from my memory: after the war I could no longer understand any written or spoken Lithuanian, and I certainly could not speak it. What was it in my wartime experience that brought this about?"

> Visual images and words tend to run together in my memory. For example, to remember someone's name, it helps me to associate an image with it. To effectively repress—to block out—memories of traumatic experiences, it seems necessary to remove the associated words, in order to contain the emotions of fear, extreme anxiety, and the sense of impending doom connected to them. But if this is so, then why did I not only retain but even increase my knowledge of the German language as a result of my ghetto and concentration camp experiences? The memories of many of these experiences were also repressed, but the German language associated with them was not. What is the difference?[1]

One explanation, he tells us, "is that being able to communicate with the Germans in concentration camps was essential to my survival. But knowing Lithuanian was, at least for me, not relevant to my survival efforts." Essentially, as Schalkowsky points out, his survival depended on avoidance of Lithuanians.

Schalkowsky, when he retired from his work in engineering, volunteered at the United States Holocaust Memorial Museum and was given the assignment to create a finding aid, inventory, and description for researchers of a document written in Yiddish by members of the Kovno Ghetto Jewish police in the Kovno Ghetto from 1941–43. This history was part of some thirty thousand pages assembled by the Jewish ghetto police which had been buried and not discovered until the sixties. Despite the fact that the Kovno Ghetto was burned to the ground by the retreating Nazis, these documents and others survived. As Sam Schalkowsky had been in the Kovno Ghetto, what he read in these documents was extremely personal. It would be years before they would become available. A copy was finally obtained by the USHMM in 1998.

As he read through these documents, Sam was reminded of the outbursts on the street and his "fear of being dragged out" and killed. "Hiding in the house, I didn't see them—there are no visual memories, only the shouting in Lithuanian. The trauma of this seven-week period preceding the establishment of the ghetto is therefore predominantly connected to words spoken in Lithuanian . . . the abruptness of this stark change from a normal existence to being engulfed by the Lithuanian orgy of brutality, humiliation, and the slaughter . . . makes my complete repression of the Lithuanian language seem understandable."[2]

"What did I learn about memory?" Schalkowsky asks. "Memory is adjustable." He speaks of traumatic affect without a specific memory attached to it, and the converse, a specific memory without the accompanying emotional affect.

A man with a meticulous memory, Sam, when comparing his experience of a specific event involving the fate of a small child with that of his companions, remembers the event and its outcome differently. He describes what he calls the "modification of the gate," not only for the past and past memory, but for what is actually permitted to be taken in now, today—a kind of vigilance that does not permit certain kinds of information to be experienced or even to gain entry. "Not only do you have to rid yourself of the images, but of the language which might contain the images."

Masha Wolpe Baras, fluent in eleven languages, and with intact memory of Aktions, selections, forced marches, completely lost Lithuanian by the end of the war. Another survivor who has lost his knowledge of Lithuanian speaks of having heard Lithuanian spoken—but not being able to see the Lithuanian collaborator—as Jewish neighbors in an adjoining room were taken away. He describes the language on the other side of the wall as the "agent of death."

Zev Birger writes in *No Time for Patience: My Road from Kaunas to Jerusalem* that during the period following the Children's Aktion in Kaunas, he would secretly leave the Ghetto and observe

> the reaction of the Lithuanians when they saw the columns of Jewish workers moving through the streets. . . . I was shocked not only by their conduct after the invasion of the Germans, but also by the fact that the Lithuanian and Ukrainian units did the dirty work for the SS. I was so deeply and lastingly shocked by the inhumane, almost animalistic conduct of the Lithuanians that a short time after the war I discovered I was no longer fluent in Lithuanian. Suddenly I could no longer utter sentences in the language that I had spoken as well as my mother tongue. Worried that there was something very wrong with my brain, I went to a doctor who determined that I had suffered such a shock from my observations outside the ghetto, that a mental block now paralyzed my memory, preventing me from recalling this language. I have never since tried to master Lithuanian again.[3]

3

Here is a boy, a teenager who, in the middle of the night, is ordered along with his father to the basement of their apartment building on Laisvės Alėja (Freedom Way) in Kaunas. All the men and boys are shot.[4] The boy, Leiser, is also shot but lies still, and when the bedlam is over he rises up and seeks help. A short time later, all survivors are forced to leave their homes and go to the ghetto. After helping his mother deliver his infant brother in the ghetto, he must then bury the infant a few days later. He witnesses the burning to death of his younger brother in a hospital where all the doctors, nurses, and patients are killed in this way. He survives the ghetto and is taken to Dachau Concentration Camp. He somehow manages to survive Dachau, but for more than a year is in a hospital with tuberculosis. When he finally is released, he describes his first experience after the war going to the sea:

When I went into the sea, I saw a sea of blood. In Spain, I wanted to paint. I would paint only blood. Is something wrong with me? No. I was in Spain. In Palanga. In school. I was with the school in Palanga. An excursion. A few days, I was never to the seaside. Only Palanga. Then to Spain. I was so dirty. I have a feeling I have to wash myself three hndred times. It was not normal. In the first flat, no warm water, no shower, no real bed, a camping bed. First time I had a feeling, a sea of blood with dead people. Then it went away. Then I enjoyed it. A holiday in Spain and Italy. Mostly, I kept everything in order.[5]

4

On October 28, 1941, a selection was made in the Kovno Ghetto, and over the next day 9,200 Jews were forced to walk to the Ninth Fort where they were all killed. Shalom Eilati, a child in the Ghetto, witnessed the solemn march and heard gunfire:

> It surprised me to realize that this road, which was visible to all as it rose diagonally from left to right, was already mostly full of people. Had I not looked up to find the source of the gunfire, their march would have been completely unheard and undetected. . . . And then, only then, did the data from my sight and hearing come together in my mind. . . . I suppose that my childhood ended right then—its innocence, the privilege of being unafraid.[6]

This became known as the Great Aktion. Afterward, whenever Eilati saw a diagonal line—in a painting or in his line of vision—or heard the sounds of multiple footsteps, he was taken back to that moment in the Ghetto, not as a distant memory but as if he were there.

Many years later, Shalom Eilati was in Washington, D.C., pursuing his studies, when he decided to visit the White House. As one group would wend its way to the entrance, another would exit the building.

They moved quietly. "Surprised, I found I was choking anew, after so many years, at the scene of the big Aktion in Democrats' Square. Shocked and upset, I left the place immediately, in turmoil."⁷

In November 1995 in Jerusalem, after the assassination of Yitzhak Rabin, Eilati joined thousands who had come to say farewell. "As for me," Eilati tells us, "as soon as I began waiting in the silent crowd, a feeling of suffocation fell upon me, of deep oppression, that grew as I moved forward in line, as though fifty-four years and one week had not gone by since the big Aktion. I turned around and went home. . . . Sometimes it seems as if a part of me is still unsure that I was saved, as if it is ready for the bubble of time allotted to me to burst."⁸

In a talk that he gave at Yad Vashem in recent years, Eilati tells about a fictional movie in which a baby from outer space lands on earth inside a capsule made of a special metal. A farmer takes him home and raises him as his own child, but the child still holds a piece of that metal from out of this world. It is forever in his pocket, marking his unique identity.

> And so we, too, the child survivors who have been returned, parachuted into the existential world in which we now live. There is this piece imprinted in us, which sets us forever apart from those around us, and even seems to be bequeathed—to our sorrow—unto our children. Even if you try—try very hard—to be "like everyone else"—you will never again be "like them," despite all your efforts. For the effort is great and the attempts are many but in fact, each of us is at any given moment a kind of secret agent, living a double life in the full sense of the word. There is the outward "normal" life, reflected in the office, on the street, in the family; and the other, hidden deep under seven seals, which you endeavor to peer at only in the dark of night, associate with as little as possible, for the sake of your sanity and functioning.⁹

Eilati notes that "[o]f the approximately 5,000 Jewish children under the age of 14 in the city of Kaunas (Kovno) before the war, 150 children survived."¹⁰ The Kinder Aktion took place in 1944 (though the killing of children and adults in more than two hundred villages occurred at

Memorial to the Children of Kovno

the beginning of the German occupation in 1941). His mother decided that on her way to forced labor, she would arrange for him to go into hiding with a Lithuanian family. They crossed the river on a boat with others; his mother removed his two Jewish stars, and instructed him that without stopping or looking back, once they reached the opposite bank, he was to cross the road and go up a path into the hill beyond. He would be met by a woman who would give him instructions. All went well except he was not met on the path by anyone. He continued walking. Then suddenly a woman whispered that he should continue up the path and she would advise him. Eventually he found himself in the house of an elderly Lithuanian woman named Julija.[11] "Like Moses,"

Eilati writes, "in the bulrushes I was cast by Mother onto the shore of life, my mother, who gave me life twice, but was unable to save her own even once."[12]

Eilati, now in Israel, describes his role:

> On urgent reserve duty, gliding like an albatross, gazing like a hawk from an immense height. . . . For years I have been deciphering military aerial photographs. Like ancient diviners examining the liver of a young calf, I bend over the stereoscope, examining the minute clues sketched in the emulsion of the film before me. Like those haruspices, I look for signs and portents, trying to prognosticate events before they materialize. Thus I can be on constant lookout, observing the horizon for events still beyond it, know in advance things that may happen before too long. As I have said, I no longer like surprises.[13]

In this way, he gains a degree of mastery over danger.

In the writing of his book *Crossing the River*—over a period of twenty years—Eilati is able to find a means to confront what has lived in him since childhood. Eilati describes early attempts at telling this story but eventually discovers a method: "[F]ind the place where there were fewer land mines, and there try placing the foot. Not in chronological order . . . not by topic. Not by force, but by association only, while listening constantly for signals from the soul—did it want, or did it not want, the next subject." The soul, he tells us, "had no end of hesitations and resistance." The strategy involved "patient circling while persistently reducing the 'no trespassing' areas. As if manufacturing dynamite. Piece by piece, patch after patch, in order to avoid creating an explosion you cannot withstand." The advantage, he notes, is that "things could become ripe in you, terrors that you brought out yesterday, to tame them and introduce them gradually into your conscious world."[14]

Judith Herman, in *Trauma and Recovery*, writes:

> Traumatic reactions occur when action is of no avail. When neither resistance nor escape is possible, the human system of self-defense becomes overwhelmed and disorganized. Each component of the ordinary response to danger, having lost

its utility, tends to persist in an altered and exaggerated state long after the actual danger is over. Traumatic events produce profound and lasting changes in physiological arousal, emotion, cognition, and memory. Moreover, traumatic events may sever these normally integrated functions from one another. The traumatized person may experience intense emotion but without clear memory of the event, or may remember everything in detail but without emotion. [As noted earlier in the words of Sam Schalkowsky] She may find herself in a constant state of vigilance and irritability without knowing why. Traumatic symptoms have a tendency to become disconnected from their source and to take on a life of their own.[15]

Dr. Herman goes on to characterize post-traumatic stress disorder in three main categories: hyperarousal—the persistent expectation of danger; intrusion—the indelible imprint of the traumatic moment; and constriction—the numbing response of surrender.

We see this today in our returning veterans. We can barely imagine the effects on Syrians living under the constant siege of life-threatening bombing and war, for the children transported during their most formative years into this nightmare of constant and insidious danger.

5

How would neuroscientists look at these effects of trauma and their formations? People such as Joseph LeDoux, Bessel van der Kolk, Antonio R. Damasio, or Mark Solms? How might we explore the integration of the neurobiological, psychological, sociocultural perspectives with material drawn from oral histories?

Sigmund Freud, in 1890, completed work on the "Project," a neuroscientific view of mind/consciousness/memory. At the time, the tools in the neurosciences were not sufficient to probe deeply enough to produce observations and results that included subjective observation that could be made available through psychoanalysis and the related approaches. The Project was abandoned and never published in Freud's lifetime. Alexander Luria, the Russian psychologist, picked up this thread in the early twentieth century, but it is only today that we have the remarkable tools in neuroscience—functional MRIs and other methods of imaging—to really begin to bridge the fields of subjective and objective mental activity. In the work of Mark Solms, expertly trained in both psychoanalysis and neuroscience, we find a pathway toward synthesis of these fields.

Antonio R. Damasio, professor and director of the Brain and Creativity Institute at the University of Southern California, said in an interview with *The Harvard Brain* (Spring 2001):

> What we really want to understand, the relation between brain systems and complex cognition and behavior, can only be explained satisfactorily by a comprehensive blend of theories and facts related to all the levels of organization of the nervous system, from molecules, and cells and circuits, to large-scale systems and physical and social environments. For almost any problem that is worth one's interest, theory and evidence from all of these levels are, in one way or another, relevant to the understanding of physiology or pathology. Since none of us can possibly practice or dominate knowledge across all of those levels, it follows that one must practice one or two very well, and be very humble about considering the rest, that is, evidence from those other levels that you do not practice. In other words, beware of explanations that rely on data from one single level, whatever the level may be.[16]

In the area of memory—how we have come to think about the formation, encoding, and retrieval of memory and the unique character of traumatic memory—scientists from many areas, using their distinct knowledge, have come together to explore this powerful subject.

We are tempted to think of memory as that which we experience entering the brain's library, as it were, and coming whole cloth onto the appropriate shelf or location, like a book to be reached for when needed later on, ready and willing and still completely intact. Such a view loses sight of the remarkable plasticity of the brain and complexity beyond our imagining.

Jorge Luis Borges's "Library at Babel"[17] gets at this in his narrator's declaration that the Library contained all books, "the minutely detailed history of the future, the archangels' autobiographies, the faithful catalogue of the Library . . . false catalogues . . . the true story of your death, the translation of every book in all languages . . ." Extravagant happiness about this eventually gave way to depression concerning books that were inaccessible. His narrator resolves the problem by suggesting that letters and symbols—like DNA—should be juggled until by chance they constructed themselves into canonical works, a kind of newly created world brought into being by chance. This enormous library is neither efficient nor has it the needed flexibility to be useful. On the other hand, perhaps he was forecasting the remarkable simplicity of the DNA molecule, four nucleotides repeating in certain specific patterns. The basic building blocks are streamlined; yet their use is infinitely complex.

Perhaps we have held to the "library" version of brain function because it is comforting to think that we might point to a certain area of the brain and declare it the precise location of memory or emotion. Yet to examine the "cellular architecture" of the brain—to use Regina Pally's term[18]—we must consider the brain's 100 billion neurons; each neuron with its axon and dendrites making "a synaptic connection with approximately 60,000 to 100,000 other neurons; the number of possible combinations of synaptic connections . . . more than the number of positively charged particles in the known universe!" Thus, we observe the brain's ability to process essentially an infinite amount of information, and a clue to the enormous plasticity of brain function. And we have not mentioned the dramatically changed role we now see regarding the deeply important role of glial cells in particular astrocytes, once thought to be no more than support tissues, now key to understanding brain function.

Here we will explore the neurobiological and corresponding psychological bases of trauma and their effects upon memory formation and retrieval, including issues of encoding during hyperarousal, dissociation, fragmentation, repetition, repression, the limiting of consciousness, and focus on central perceptual details, as well as the limits of language to convey traumatic experience.

An important note here is the difference in interview techniques that can strongly shape the nature of responses. The most directed interviews—the Lithuanian Documentation Project where the purpose was informational rather than focused on psychological exploration, for instance—leave very little room for examining individual responses. However, much can be learned from bystanders and witnesses to trauma in the *way* that experience is remembered and told. In some cases the witnesses, following the interviews, are asked to visit the places where the actual trauma occurred, and during these visits, the affect of the interviewee quite often radically differs from that during the prior interview situation.[19]

6

One day recently, I walked out of the front door of my house to the mailbox, crossing the garden, and as I returned I heard an ominous sound—a crunching of wood breaking. Without determining its source—apart from the sure knowledge that it was above my head—I simply ran as fast as I could toward the house. It might have been wiser to look up and to determine at what angle the huge branches, torn off by the wind, would fall. But had I done so, taken the time to ascertain the full situation, it might have been too late to get out of the way of the falling branches.

Joseph LeDoux, professor at the Center of Neural Science at New York University, describes putting his "face close to the thick glass plate in front of a puff adder in the Zoological Gardens, with the firm determination of not starting back if the snake struck at me; but as soon as the blow was struck, my resolution went for nothing, and I jumped a yard or two backwards with astonishing rapidity. My will and reason were powerless against the imagination of a danger which had never been experienced."[20]

What brain functions had been called into play in these moments of potential threat? And why had his determination beforehand not prevailed when the puff adder struck, though the recipient of the attack was safely behind a plate glass barrier?

During the mid-fifties, I worked as a research assistant at Yale University School of Medicine, studying prefrontal lobe function and delayed-response memory. Paul MacLean's work in that same lab involved the limbic system. Its importance was considered a revolutionary hypothesis at that time—a system charged with maintaining the balance between the internal world and external reality, containing both innate circuitry and circuitry modifiable by experience, a system charged and concerned with emotion and instinct. It was MacLean who first coined the term *limbic* and who posited the notion of the triune brain: the primitive or reptilian brain, the intermediate or limbic brain, and the rational brain or neocortex.

Originally, this was considered a hierarchical system—brainstem and hypothalamus (regulation of internal homeostasis), limbic system (mediation between internal function and external reality) and neocortex (analysis and interaction with the external world). Later, it became clear that these systems operate in highly complex interactions. As Bessel van der Kolk notes, a "well-functioning neocortex is necessary for reasoning strategies to attain personal goals, for weighing a range of options for action, for predicting the outcome of one's actions, and for deciding which sensory stimuli are relevant and which are not. In these discriminatory functions, it is assisted by a well-functioning septo-hippocampal system."[21]

Joseph LeDoux posits the importance of the amygdala, the almond-shaped organ in the brain that appears to be the "link between all sensory systems and all fear response systems."[22] The amygdala is most clearly implicated in the evaluation of the emotional meaning of incoming stimuli.[23] LeDoux makes a distinction between emotional and cognitive processing: "[E]motional processing often leads to bodily response, whereas cognitive processing leads to more cognitive responses." The biology of these two systems differs. And in evolutionary terms, for good reason. "Emotional reactions . . . are really reactions that are important in survival situations. The advantage is that by allowing evolution to do the thinking for you first, you basically buy the time that you need to think about the situation and do the most reasonable things." LeDoux points out that freezing when danger appears is what animals and people generally do first. Yet if we had time to think about it, we might move about or run, which might cause further harm. When the bomb detonated during the Olympics in Atlanta in 1996, people hunched "over in a freezing position for a couple of seconds" and then took off running.

Another point of interest is that the "connectivity of the amygdala with the neocortex is not symmetrical. The amygdala projects back to the neo-cortex in a much stronger sense than the neo-cortex projects to the amygdala." Thus, the earlier incidents—falling tree branch and puff adder—likely induced a response from the amygdala first, getting the body into play before cognitive function had a chance to weigh the pros and cons of a proper course of action. According to LeDoux, the "amygdala's ability to control the cortex is greater than the ability of the cortex to control the amygdala," which may explain "why it's so hard for us to will away anxiety; emotions, once they're set into play, are very difficult to turn off. Hormones and other long-acting substances are released in the body during emotions. These return to the brain and tend to lock you into the state you're in at the time. Once you're in that state it's very difficult for the cortex to find a way of working its way down to the amygdala and shutting it off." Thus, says LeDoux, the difficulty of therapy. The role of the neocortex in controlling the amygdala is like "trying to find your way from New York to Boston by way of country roads rather than super highways." On the other hand, the amygdala is able to control the neocortex by arousing a number of areas in a nonspecific way.

Another way to think of this is as follows: "The amygdala is essential for decoding emotions, particularly threatening stimuli. External stimuli reach the amygdala via two different pathways, which complement each other. A short, imprecise route comes from the thalamus, which receives sensory stimuli and allows us to prepare for potential danger before knowing exactly what the danger is. A longer, more precise route comes from the medial prefrontal cortex, the area of the brain that is involved in the final phase of fear, in which the brain reacts to danger and chooses a course of action."[24]

Thus, extreme trauma and the response to it may be more deeply embedded and less under the control of cognitive processes, and may surface in memory in powerful and unbidden forms. What would have been appropriate responses to danger initially are no longer warranted when the danger has subsided; yet it is not possible to close off the response. At a later point, the occurrence of anything suggestive of the original experience is capable of eliciting "profound fear responses by reactivating these powerfully potentiated amygdala circuits."[25]

Some contemporary examples might serve to illustrate this phenomenon: In 1970, when I started teaching at the university, my first students were men returning from the war in Vietnam. They were, in general, unrehabilitated; some were heavily addicted to drugs; some appeared to be in shock, still dazed by the world they had recently left. One veteran always stood at the back of the hallway, nearest the stairway, while we waited for the preceding class to leave the classroom. It was as if he needed to be sure he had a clear escape route. I had not known the details of his experience in Vietnam, until after an assignment reading Dante's *Inferno*. He dropped by my office one afternoon and handed me a packet, telling me that he had not been able to talk about his experience in Vietnam, nor to write about it until now, that Dante and the descent into the Inferno had given him a route for his expression. He asked that I read his writing and I told him that I would as soon as I had time to do so. Of course, I took the pages home that same evening and read every word. What I learned was that he had been part of a special reconnaissance group that took the forward positions which put him and his men in grave danger. That he was, at a certain point, airlifted into a helicopter from a ring of fire. That men in his unit had been killed. That he could identify a tripwire fine as a hair that might be attached to explosives. That when he saw the film *Platoon,* and came to the part where the American soldiers in Vietnam found a metal box and began to open it, he screamed in the movie theater for them to stop; he knew it would contain explosives. He described the terrible longing they had to find signs of the enemy, to touch something the enemy had used. He was tuned to danger, at the ready to read whatever environment he was in for the least sign that might require sudden action for survival. This hypervigilance endured even though he was now safe in America and its necessity was no longer required.

During the Iraq war, a young man on a brief army leave comes home to America and goes to a shopping mall with his family. He describes his terrible unease, that he is without his machine gun, that no one is guarding the entrances and exits of the mall, that people are moving about in large numbers and no one seems concerned. In Iraq, every face and motion must be interpreted. His life depended on this knowledge. He speaks of being afraid that he will feel this terror and the need for vigilance for the rest of his life.

A woman who survived as a child during World War II by hiding in the sewers beneath Lvov, Poland, for fourteen months, lived in a tube five feet high by four feet wide amid sewage and sewer rats. When asked how that experience manifests itself in her present-day life, she describes visiting a new house and feeling fearful about going down to the basement. But then, when exploring the attic, she thinks immediately that this might be a good place to hide. She points out how hard it is, after living on instinct during those years, to feel free of the need to do so. Cognitive function assures her that she is safe and the earlier need to fear for her life is no longer necessary. Yet the ingrained emotional response says otherwise.[26]

Shalom Eilati describes a memory from his childhood in the Kovno Ghetto. The morning after a selection that took 9,200 people to their deaths, he is walking in the square where the selection had taken place when he comes upon "strangely shaped lumps among the mounds of rubbish."[27] When he draws near, he realizes that these are dead bodies. Ever after, he is transported back there by a series of triggers, including music.

> Mahler's First Symphony, for instance, the second and third movements: first a slow funeral march, accompanied by deep rhythmic drumbeats against a background of a meandering Jewish tune—and I cringe, accompanying the marchers' slow progress up the hill. Then suddenly, after a brief silence a paralyzing scream bursts out from dozens of instruments, and I choke in tears, hold my head in desperation and cannot be consoled. I am there.[28]

Here we can observe a number of aspects of traumatic memory: the triggers that enable us to gain access to memory; the ways that memory is encoded in multiple sites and is constructed and retrieved through a series of operations—hormonal, neuronal, the action of neurotransmitters. And as Bessel van der Kolk has observed, we begin to see how the body remembers.

When he visited the concentration camp Dachau and walked into the barracks that had been reconstructed, Sam Schalkowsky describes "seeing the wooden planks that made me itch." Walking by the Dachau Crematorium "brought back the smell," brought back the experience in Stutthof Concentration Camp, where he was forced to clean up after the killings in the crematorium there.

Prior to being interviewed by the Shoah Foundation, Masha Wolpe Baras began to hunger for bread, as she had hungered in the concentration camp for the small ration of bread prisoners were allotted, insufficient for survival. For several weeks, she ate little else but bread, a literal repetition of the earlier situation in extremis.

Chapter VIII

Rescue

Know you a piece of earth where no person was killed?
Here they were killed. But here I survived.

—Yocheved Cartok Inčiūrienė

1

This small "piece of earth" called Lithuania has known its share of battles, occupations, and killing fields. Perhaps there is no place in the world, as Yocheved Inčiūrienė tells us, that does not contain the remnants of lives caught in war and terror and betrayal. As noted earlier, what happened here has many versions. We must ask which ones make legitimate claim.

When the Russians invaded Lithuania in 1940 and exiled many Lithuanians to Siberia and later, when the Germans broke the nonaggression pact they had made with Russia and invaded Lithuania and instigated the majority of the killing of Jews, those Lithuanians who sought to help by hiding Jews did so believing that the German occupation was to be permanent. They did not have the hindsight of the fall of the Third Reich. Thus, those who risked their lives, the lives of their families, and their communities had immense courage in the face of enormous and unending threat. And many who helped were in fact imprisoned, exiled, and murdered. Even in the cases where Jews were hidden for a certain period and when later the pressure and risk became too great for the rescuers and the Jews were asked to leave, attempts were made by some to locate other hiding places for them. In one particular case, when the situation became increasingly dangerous a rescuer of a young mother and infant asked the woman to leave and suggested that, as the weather was still warm in September and the waters of the river still warm, she might drown herself and the baby. When the moment came and the woman walked away with her baby, the rescuer went after her and brought her back, but she never forgave herself for her momentary lapse of courage.[1]

The Vilna Gaon Jewish State Museum of Lithuania has published a series of books called *Hands Bringing Life and Bread*, honoring a number of these Righteous Among the Nations. As urgent as it is to understand what causes extreme and murderous brutality, it is equally important to understand what permits some among us to put aside self-concern and self-interest in order to provide help when it is needed. Ona Šimaitė was one such person. It was no simple matter to rescue: it took ingenuity, the ability to read complex situations and make immediate responses. Whether through her persistence, her ability to play roles, to appear uninformed, to wait out her interrogators, to ignore her own fear, she was exceptional, and still she paid a high price. From this one life, we have much to learn. Though she was eventually arrested by the Gestapo in 1944 and tortured, she never gave any information to her torturers. She was deported to Dachau and subsequently to the Lidelange Concentration Camp in France, which was eventually liberated by the Allies. She saved children and adults, and rescued valuable documents and manuscripts as well. After the war she kept promises to those who did not survive, contacting their families with their last messages. She lived in near poverty for the remainder of her life. Abba Kovner, leader of the Resistance in the Vilna Ghetto, once said that "if there are ten righteous among the nations, Ona Simaite is one of them."[2] As of January 1, 2018, some 893 Lithuanians have been awarded the Yad Vashem Medal of the Righteous Among the Nations.

2

During the years 1942–44 of the German occupation, some 250 infants and children were taken to the Lopšelis Children's Home in Vilijampolė (near to the Kovno Ghetto) and, of these, 120 Jewish infants and children were rescued. Dr. Petras Baublys—born in 1914 and killed in 1974 in an airplane crash—served as physician there during that time. He risked his own and his family's lives to save Jewish children, along with Dr. E. Kurklietienė-Žemkalnienė and nurses Marcelė Jasaitytė, Apolonija Grigaliūnaitė-Pažemeckienė, Efinija Butkutė, and Pranciška Vitonytė.[3] During these years, Jewish women in the Kovno (Kaunas) Ghetto were forbidden by the Germans to bear children.

What in the history or nature of an individual might account for later acts of rescue and heroism? Here is a description of the first day of medical school for Dr. Baublys. Many of the students had come from villages and, wearing their best clothes, entered the classroom shyly, feeling intimidated. "Suddenly, in walked a short, slender young man. He was wearing a colorful shirt but no coat, multicolored golfing slacks, rather worn sport shoes, and carried a fishing rod. He confidently strode past the front desk and remarked in a voice full of irony: 'Here we are! We are going to be colleagues!'" At first the others thought he had lost his way. But no, this was Petras Baublys. After the professor left the room, Baublys announced that he "still had to do some fishing!"

He attracted the attention of the others, always arriving on time, in good humor, ready with an amusing story. He took few notes but listened attentively and seemed to retain everything. During recesses, he would entertain the others with Charlie Chaplin imitations.

Later, under great pressure, he was compassionate and sensitive to others. "Petitions from ghetto residents to accept children were never rejected. When the doorbell rang at night, the door was opened to reveal a living bundle. Some were infants, some two- or three-year-old toddlers, accompanied by baskets containing toys. One can imagine how tragic was the existence of parents living in the ghetto, who sent forth their children on an unknown journey."[4] Members of the Gestapo began to notice the increase in the number of orphans after Dr. Baublys began working at the Children's Home. They increased their visits, interrogations, and document checks. At one point when the Gestapo had come to interrogate, a quick-thinking nurse prepared a roasted goose dinner with Cognac and all the trimmings. By the time the dinner was finished, the Gestapo no longer needed to pursue their original purpose. The work was very dangerous and Jewish male infants who had been circumcised were in particular danger. Others did not speak Lithuanian as their primary language. Homes had to be found for them quickly.

Petras Baublys was usually the first to discern when a colleague was in distress and to offer help. Though the youngest of his colleagues, he excelled in his work. His nurse at Lopšelis, Pranciška Vitonytė, "told for years that respect and love for Dr. Baublys enabled her to bear the hardships of the work and to conquer fear when interrogated by the Gestapo."

In 1977, Dr. Baublys was posthumously awarded the title "Righteous Among the Nations" by Yad Vashem. His brother Sergejus and sister-in-law Yadvyga were also recognized for hiding a Jewish child in their home. A brother, Rostis Baublys, accepted the award on behalf of his family, saying, "They did what every decent person ought to do everywhere at all times."

In 1994, a commemoration took place in Kaunas, and some of those rescued as children returned from around the world to Lopšelis to honor Dr. Baublys. During this time, I had occasion to interview two of the nurses who had worked there during the war and to talk at length with Dr. Elena Miknevičienė, his former classmate and colleague. What made this unusual man able to provide compassion and help when it was urgently needed? Did his ability to go against the grain, his seemingly innate independence, the wit to carry a fishing rod into the first day of

Dr. Elena Miknevečienė, colleague of Dr. Baublys

medical school, provide any clues to his later willingness to risk his life on behalf of others? And to do so in a way that provided the least risk to those who worked alongside him at Lopšelis?

It is to be hoped that others will take up the challenge, to explore the qualities of character and psychological makeup and life experience that permit and prepare one to put aside risk and help others, as was done in the town of Le Chambon in France, for instance, by all who inhabited that place. Of those rescuers whom I have interviewed in Lithuania, none believed that what they had done was out of the ordinary.

3

One remarkable person, Bronius Elijošaitis (born in 1922), along with his mother and father, helped to save a number of people in Lithuania,

Bronius Elijošaitis, who helped to rescue Yocheved Cartok Inčiūrienė and whose mother was instrumental in saving her life

including Yocheved Inčiūrienė. During one of my interviews with him, after several hours I asked if he was troubled by all of my questions. He laughed and reminded me: "I was interrogated by the Gestapo. And more than once! Do you think *you* can make me afraid?"

A putsch in the town of Tauragė in 1927, where the family lived at the time, resulted in killings and Bronius's father sought refuge in Germany. Bronius, at the age of five, was imprisoned with his mother in Šiauliai, Lithuania, and later they were brought to a concentration camp in Varniai. During that time Bronius became ill with diphtheria and nearly died. An American emigrants' newspaper wrote an article about this and he and his mother were let go. For a short while they joined his father in Germany, but eventually returned to Lithuania. [5]

What is worth noting, in the case of Yocheved Inčiūrienė, is the number of people who risked their lives to save her, the extraordinary difficulty of keeping even a single person alive. "When the Germans occupied Kaunas, Yocheved Čartokaitė was locked in the ghetto. On the first occasion, in the autumn of 1941, she escaped from there."[6] She had no money or belongings and was hidden by various friends and students, including Bronius Elijošaitis. His parents, Ona and Pranas Eliošaičiai,

Yocheved Cartok Inčiūrienė

accepted her and provided her with a student certificate in the name of Marytė Šimukėnaitė. They organized others who would hide her, including poet Kazys Jakūbėnas, Zofija Paulauskienė, Jonas and Valerija Stepaičiai, Jonas Adomavičius, Feliksas Molskis, Vladas Mongirdas, and others. Yocheved told me that when she first entered the home of Bronius Elijošaitis, his mother sat her down for several hours and talked with her, giving her guidelines for how she was to live in such a way that she might survive. His mother condemned the genocide by the Germans and the "White Armbanders" (members of the LAF, Lithuanian Activist Front) and offered to help as much as she could. Bronius's mother explained the rules of the conspiracy and how to behave in extreme situations of arrest and interrogation.[7] Yocheved felt in retrospect that this gave her the most possibility to live. It included not staying in any one place for more than a night or two; betrayal by a neighbor was likely.

The family hid others, including a leader of the anti-Nazi movement in Lithuania. Bronius's mother "was arrested for this and imprisoned in the ward of prisoners sentenced to death." In January 1944, she was deported without trial to Germany for hard labor, but escaped and returned to Lithuania.

At a certain point, it became too dangerous for Yocheved to remain in Kaunas.

"I thought that I don't want to remain in the ghetto." When she and her sister and mother attempted initially to escape to Russia at the start of the war, they went forty kilometers but had to return. "I could not leave my mother. But in the ghetto there was a father, sister, grandparents. But where must I stay? I was at one house, a second, one night, two nights, but it was dangerous. But one time I decided to go out. While hiding, partisans came to the door: 'Was here a Jewish girl?' I cannot stay here. I walk out. They either shoot me or not."[8]

Yocheved is caught and taken to the German administration building and beaten.

"Were you afraid?"

"I was very angry. Why he beats me? Then they took me to the second floor, to the manager of the station. The German said: 'You want to run away from the ghetto?'

"No, I have hunger. And I want to eat. You gave us no bread." [Yocheved tells this with a hearty laugh.]

Then she is taken to another place with a different guard and is beaten with a belt. She runs around the room to get away from him but he continues to beat her. She spies a guard through the door who is laughing.

"I was so angry. I said in German, 'Why do you laugh?'

"I ran away from the ghetto twelve times. Once I was gone for several days in December. My grandfather was very angry. He said, 'You must not run away. All Jews must be together. It will come, the Messiah, on a white horse, and we will all be free.' He took away from me those things that would give me the ability to run away—my snow shoes, coat."

On December 20, 1941, Yocheved left the Kovno Ghetto and did not return. She stayed with various friends and learned that the brother of a friend lived on a large farm outside of Kaunas and perhaps would agree to hide her. He was to come to Kaunas on the fifteenth of January, 1942, with a sleigh and two horses.

Yocheved tells that "when he came, he dressed me in a large sheepskin coat, placed me in a sleigh with a cover of straw to hide me. I was very afraid. Someone will ask: 'Where are you going? Who is that girl?'"

They traveled and got lost; ten hours passed. And in that way Yocheved went away from Kaunas.

Jonas Saunoris, rescuer

They arrived in Mankiškiai. Jonas Saunoris's parents had been exiled to Siberia in 1941, his brother Edmund had been arrested and disappeared. At the time of the German occupation, Jonas returned to his father's estate.

"Jonas Saunoris accepted me like a member of his family and guarded me like a true sister. This way I lived until the end of 1942."[9]

Yocheved was discovered by a visit from the shoemaker's wife from Kaunas and knew that she must immediately leave Mankiškiai.

Jonas Saunoris moved to Poland in 1944 and later to Canada, working as a scientist/biologist. Yocheved wished to honor him as a Righteous Among the Nations at Yad Vashem but had lost touch with him. After many months of searching, I discovered that he had passed away.

A document from Yad Vashem, dated December 24, 1993, contains the following:

> Report concerning Mrs. Marytė (Šimukėnaitė) Inčiūrienė, Place: Lithuania, Time: 1942–1943. It happened fifty-two (52) years ago during the Christmas and New Year Holidays—In the autumn of 1941 in Lithuania, under German occupation, the Jews were rounded [up] and shot to death.
>
> My family was deported to Siberia by Soviets, and I was forced to take the administration of our family farm—in spite that I wanted very much to study at the university.
>
> At the end of 1941, I came to Kaunas (a city in Central Lithuania) to have a minor operation. After a successful care in hospital, I was declared being fit to leave hospital on even of the Christmas—52 years ago exactly.
>
> During the first week of 1942 I have visited in Kaunas my friend, Adomavičius, Jonas, and mentioned to him that I would like to have some person—on our farm—who could teach me the foreign languages: German and English, which would compensate my impossibility to attend the university. He suggested to me that I, returning from operation to our farm, should bring home a Jew, who was hiding in Kaunas and visited my friend—an intelligent girl who could teach me these two languages.
>
> I agreed, and brought that Jewish girl from Kaunas to our farm (150 kilometres north of Kaunas) by horses and sled, somewhere in mid-January, 1942.

That Jewish girl was Marytė Šimukėnaitė—according to the forged high school identification card that she had with her.

And on the farm, in Mankiškiai, I allowed her to move freely, not hiding, open—telling only to my intimate friends that she was Jewish.

And that was very dangerous for me, because several of my neighbours have suspected that she was Jewish, and the slightest denunciation to the local police would be the death sentence for myself personally to be shot by death squad. Maryte Šimukėnaitė remained on our family farm—under conditions described above—from January 1942 to about early spring 1943—when she was married to Jurgis Inčiūra.

During that time was impossible for me to continue lessons in German and English because administration of the farm took all my attention.

The presence of Maryte Šimukėnaitė on our family farm in Mankiškiai was very dangerous for me, but helped to save the life of that Jewish girl. I remember very well, even today, three incidents related to her presence in my home, namely: 1) In mid-winter, the local police sneaked into our family and shot—in front of my house—our last dog. Both of us became very afraid of that incident and we both fled immediately. I—for several hours—to a nearby forest to hide, and Marytė Šimukėnaitė was hidden for several hours that day with one family of my farm workers. Late that day we returned to our house apartments—both very shaken from fright. 2) In mid-summer 1942, in order to appease the mounting pressure, I have sent Marytė Šimukėnaitė and Jonas Adomavičius (who was vacationing at that time in my house in Mankiškiai) with two horses, wagon and driver to attend the holy mass at the Catholic church in Saukotas (church town located five kilometers from our place in Mankiškiai). I had hope that attendance of the Catholic Mass in Catholic Parish church would eliminate the suspicion of my neighbours that she is Jewish.

That faked act helped but did not eliminate the suspicion entirely, that Marytė Šimukėnaitė is Jewish. And I have evidence for that, namely, see page 4 of that letter.

In spring 1943, after Marytė Šimukėnaitė married Jurgis Inčiūra at Catholic church in Saukotas, the priest of that church (who administered on them the rites of Catholic marriage) has stopped me and asked me: "Is that right, what people are saying, that Marytė Šimukėnaitė I have recently married, is in truth a Jew?" I denied that to that priest.[10]

You see, Mrs. Gusarova [official at Yad Vashem], the situation was very stressful, very dangerous for my own life. What matters, is the fact that I helped to save the life of a Jewish girl, Marytė Šimukėnaitė, in very dangerous conditions.

And I have saved her life without any anticipation of profit from that.

—Jean Saunoris, Montreal, December 24, 1993, Christmas Eve, Peace on Earth for the people of good will![11]

Yocheved Cartok Inčiūrienė said many times that she did not understand why her friend Yanina should live and she should not: "I could not believe it is forbidden for me to go out on the street, or to the cinema, yet my friends could. I was sure that I must live a life. I did not believe that I will perish. I must live. Even in the forest when a bomb exploded, I said to myself, this is not for me."

I asked Yocheved if she had ever imagined how her life might have gone, had she taken the early opportunity to save herself, yet endangering her mother and sister?

"No, I never thought about it. It is impossible to think 'What would be if . . . ?' I am living in the present. In the past I never lived."

4

The daughter of the mayor of a small village in the mountains of Greece once wrote to me: "Do we not all take the sun from the same yard?" And Simonas Davidavičius, director of the Sugihara Museum in Kaunas, Lithuania, when I commented on the degree of killing that had taken place in Lithuania asked: "Have you no bones under your bed?" They were speaking of our common humanity and our shared responsibility.

As ferocious and powerful as the tragedies we humans inflict upon one another are, the deeds of ordinary people who take it upon themselves to save and rescue others with no thought of recompense while putting themselves in harm's way, can serve as our finest teachers. Each act is unique.

And there are those who become our teachers. What motivates a young man, born after the war, during the silence of the Soviet regime, whose own family was exiled to Siberia, to become the voice to speak for the Kėdainiai Jewish Community and its heritage as director of the Kėdainiai Regional Museum? And in 2011, for Rimantas Žirgulis to create a commemoration, via the museum along with the Kėdainiai municipality, of the seventieth anniversary of the Holocaust on August 28, "for our lost co-citizens in the Old Market Square near the complex of synagogues"?

Rimantas Žirgulis, director of the Kėdainiai Regional Museum

Keidan Massacre Place Memorial 2011

And in September of that year, an unveiling of a memorial near the mass grave of Kėdainiai—a steel wall created by an artist with the family names of those 2,076 Jewish souls who were killed there from the towns of Šėta, Žeimiai, and Kėdainiai?

As Rimantas wrote to me in 2011, he was the great-grandchild, grandson, son, and brother of deportees from June 14, 1941:

> So, in my family are four generations of deportees who were sent to Siberia. My father with my grandfather, grandmother and my uncle were deported to Isles of Trofimovsk and Bobrovsk in the delta of the Lena River in the far North. They spent sixteen years there and lost one child, the brother of my father who died of disease. . . . But very few Lithuanians were thinking about the fate of their Jewish neighbors who could not exit from the mass graves. I am an historian. I feel as a citizen of Kėdainiai my duty to talk about our history and contemporary problems. So for me it is very important to commemorate the whole community, for our citizens who lived here about three hundred years. And probably the main lesson for Lithuanians should be to finish dividing the society into "we" and "they," which is why I am going to write all names and family names in Lithuanian.

Žirgulis's purpose has been not only to commemorate the Holocaust in Lithuania but to teach about the presence of the Jewish community for centuries before in the town of Kėdainiai. For here was the place where the Gaon of Vilnius, born in 1721, came to study as a child. His knowledge was so exceptional—from the entire corpus of Jewish writings to mathematics, astronomy, science, music, philosophy, and linguistics. It is said that he first studied with a Rav, but that by the age of seven he was so immensely knowledgeable and devoted to study that he continued on his own. And it was here where the great thinker and scholar, Moshe-Leib Lilienblum was born in 1843. Lilienblum advocated establishing a closer connection between religion and life. After various riots, he began to think about national independence and to abide by the notion of *Haskalah*, enlightenment.

Jewish Cheder, Kėdainiai, now destroyed

Schools in Kėdainiai included the Hebrew Elementary School of the Tarbut network, Yiddish schools, a cheder of the Yavne network. The small wooden cheder was still present when I first visited Keidan, but was later taken down. In Kėdainiai there were seven prayer houses prior to World War I, as well as Torah Study societies, Mishna Societies, Ein YaAkov, and Chevra Chadishas. Hashomer HaTzair was established in the 1920s, and Betar. It is important to know that Kėdainiai was a multicultural town comprising six ethnic and religious communities during the seventeenth and eighteenth centuries.

Rimantas Žirgulis has opened an exposition in the former shul of the Jewish community there, commemorating the lost Jewish community of Keidan. His real effort has been to create a permanent exhibition depicting the prewar Jewish community and to provide ongoing educational programs for teachers and students and visitors from all over the world about this community. Here, in his own words, are his thoughts about growing up during Soviet times, and what led him to make the life choices that are so important and that provide a model for all of us.

5

Myra Sklarew: Year and place of your birth?

Rimantas Žirgulis: April seventh, nineteen sixty-seven, Kėdainiai Town.

M. S.: Nature and history of your family? How many generations were born in Lithuania and which villages and towns?

R. Z.: My grandparents and great grandparents with family name Žirgulis (from my grandfather side) and Lukošius (from my grandmother side) lived in Lažai village and surroundings of Surviliškis township in Kėdainiai district. My father met and married my mother in Siberia. She was from the Siberian Kirensk town, Irkutsk region.

M. S.: Your early memories?

R. Z.: My early memories come from our old flat which my parents rented in an old wooden house built in the nineteen hundreds. And huge Soviet airplanes, which flew over our house—because a Soviet military airport was very close—and frightened me. Also they disturbed our watching TV. In nineteen seventy, my father got a new flat, two rooms in a newly built five-story house, so we moved there. Our family was large: parents, my brother Vytas, my grandmother Barbora, and I. But in nineteen seventy-two, my brother died from cancer, and in nineteen seventy-six, my grandmother, too.

M. S.: Your first awareness of the wartime history: occupation by Soviets, occupation by Germans, postwar occupation by Soviets, precautions you were required to be aware of?

R. Z.: Because I am a child of Soviet times, so my first awareness and all information about Soviet-Nazi occupations was only from the point of view of Soviet propaganda, movies, books. This topic was so often in Soviet Union and very popular among boys. My parents especially protected me from any historical truth, such as occupations, deportations, et cetera. They didn't want me to have problems in my future life and career, because sometimes children of former deportees had obstacles to enter the university. But I heard some conversations and stories about deportation and life in Siberia. Also I knew that my parents were listeners of "Voice of America," "Liberty," and other prohibited radio stations. So this is why in nineteen seventy-nine I became a very active listener of radio broadcasting about rock music. This music was my greatest hobby and helped me to forget all stupid and grey life of Soviet reality. . . . So all historical truth about the period of occupations in Lithuania I had only from nineteen eighty-eight, when the movement for independence—Sajūdis—began its activity.

M. S.: How did these occupations affect you and your family?

R. Z.: The family of my paternal grandfather was deported to Siberia during the first and most terrible, unexpected deportation on June fourteenth, nineteen forty-one. They spent sixteen years, and five of them [1942–47] in most terrible conditions far north—islands situated in the delta of Laptevy sea. They had a piece of ice instead of glass in the window of their hut. In nineteen forty-two died one brother of my father, and my grandparents lost their health and became invalids from the fishing in cold water of northern sea. My father and his brother also worked together with their parents despite they were fourteen and eight years old. . . . Sometimes my father transported bodies of dead people. . . . They have returned back home in nineteen fifty-seven, but it seems their further life was unlucky.

R. Z.: In Soviet times, I didn't know the real reasons why my family was deported, because my grandfather was not such a big farmer: he had only twenty-five hectares of land. A few years ago, I found documents of my family in the archive of the former KGB. In nineteen thirty-seven, my grandfather was a leader of the National Party (Tautininkų sąjunga) Surviliškis branch—the only official political party in Lithuania at that time. Although it was only for four months, but my grandfather was found to be among the greatest enemies of the Soviet regime in nineteen forty-one . . . So again, all meaning of tragedy I have understood only from nineteen eighty-eight.

M. S.: How was contemporary Lithuanian history taught in your schools?

R. Z.: When I was a pupil, there was almost nothing about the history of Lithuania at all; almost all history told about the history of Russia and later, the USSR. . . . Contemporary situation is the opposite.

M. S.: You have played a major role in bringing the specific history of the Jewish people of Lithuania into the light, and done so at a time when it was not fully acknowledged or even known by many. What has made you take on this controversial work?

R. Z.: First of all, why do you think it is a controversial work? I don't think so. Finally Lithuanians should cease dividing people, history, heritage, and tragedies into we and they, our and not our. . . . I am working on the commemoration of our Jews—citizens of Lithuania. . . . And when almost all our Jews are lying in the mass graves, my credo is: Who other if not me?

M. S.: Tomas Venclova speaks of knowing very little about Jewish history in Lithuania. Soviet texts didn't mention Jews at all. Mass murders were written about but not specified. Is that how it was for you?

R. Z.: Yes, Soviets prohibited mentioning of the Holocaust, so we have a few generations of Lithuanians without understanding of this tragedy and which didn't see any living Jews. Some parts of society are indifferent, some don't want to recognize this, but the March of the Living which I have seen in Molėtai on August twenty-ninth, twenty-sixteen,[12] gives me a faith that the situation is changing for the better and is not hopeless.

M. S.: Doctor Petras Baublys, head of the Lopšelis Orphanage in Viliampole during the War, took on a grave responsibility in saving Jewish babies. I had a chance to talk at length with a doctor and some of the nurses who worked with him during that time. What was it about him that allowed him to take the risks to do this?

R. Z.: There were real intellectuals, humanists, whose duty it was to help other people despite their nationality. It is a pity that at that time Lithuania had so few such personalities and so weak a civil society damaged by first Soviet and Nazi occupations.

M. S.: Have you ever been afraid in your work? How was it that you decided to become an historian?

R. Z.: I am a total humanitarian, so I had not so many options. Because history was one of my favourite topics, it is why I decided to became an historian. And I am very glad, that as a person and an historian I had the opportunity to live and to work in a very interesting and important period of Lithuania's history.

M. S.: In an ideal interview where time is not an issue, what would you like us to know about your life and work that we are unaware of?

R. Z.: I am full of nonimplemented plans and wishes, because Kėdainiai is such a wonderful place, where maybe I should spend twelve lives at the same position as museum director (as a Buddhist) and then I could implement all that I wish.

M. S.: If you had all the time, energy, and resources to do anything that you wished, what might that project/activity, lifework be? What do you envision working on in thirty years?

R. Z.: First of all, I want Lithuanians to begin to commemorate the Holocaust the same as other of our tragic dates—January thirteenth or June fourteenth. Then it was evident that we became a normal nation. . . . Next, I would like my town to become an intellectual place with main brands as Dukes Radziwills and Czeslaw Milosz. This is why I am organizing festivals in honor of Czeslaw Milosz and Radviliada [Radziwills]. Third, I would like my museum to become the most innovative, interesting, and attractive cultural institution in our region.

M. S.: What are you currently working on?

R. Z.: I am working on the project "Preserving the heritage of Dukes Radziwills in Kėdainiai and Nesvyzh," an adaptation for the tourists for the twenty-fourteen-to-twenty-twenty European Neighbourhood Instrument Cross-border Cooperation for the Latvia-Lithuania-Belarus Programme. So it is a difficult demanding, and totally time-consuming work. But the heritage of Dukes Radziwills is worth it. Also, I am implementing several other projects.

Chapter IX

Who Are Our Teachers?

1

Was it the man who took me to a town called Birštonas early in my journey to Lithuania to talk with a teacher there who had assigned her students interviews with their grandparents concerning their experiences during the war and during the Soviet occupations before and afterward? A daring task, given the years of secrecy under the Soviet occupation. And to see the few remaining wooden synagogues in distant towns? Or to talk earnestly with a stranger who had much to learn about this country of her forebears? And to generously take the time to do so when his work demands were pressing?

Saulius Beržinis founded Film Studio Kopa in 1991. The company has produced more than eighty documentary films and television programs released in Lithuania as well as the United States, France, U.K., Germany, the Netherlands, and Russia. The focus has been largely on the Holocaust during World War II, and on Jewish and Roma historical and cultural heritage in Eastern and Central Europe. Saulius Beržinis received the Humanist of the Year Award presented in 2019 by the Embassy of Finland and the Rogatchi Foundation in Lithuania.

Kopa supplies material to educational and documentary film and television programs in Lithuania and abroad, including the United States Holocaust Memorial Museum, the BBC, the Vilna Gaon Jewish State Museum of Lithuania, Yad Vashem, and other international organizations. Beržinis is founding director of the Independent Holocaust Archive of

Saulius Beržinis

Lithuania, another critically important aspect of his work. His Holocaust documentaries include *Farewell, Jerusalem of Lithuania* (1994), *The Road to Treblinka* (1997), *Yudel's Unwritten Diary* (2004), and a film on the Holocaust in Jurbarkas, which became controversial because he dared to name the killers of the Jews in that town in 1941. One of the most striking films and most important, well beyond the confines of any national borders, is *Lovely Faces of the Killers* (2002), a film where he interviews killers late in their lives. This film offers a powerful view into the psychology and motivation of killing. We may well ask why a man takes on this challenging and controversial lifework.

Saulius Beržinis Interview

Myra Sklarew: Where were you born? Your Family?

Saulius Beržinis: I was born in Vilnius, twenty-three November, nineteen fifty. My father, Viktoras Beržinis [1923–1995], was a poet and worked in the Publishing House Mintis, and also as a copyreader in the National Drama Theater, where he met my mother, Genė [Genovaitė] Jasiūnaitė [1925], a young promising actress. They married in July nineteen fifty, and I had no siblings. After my birth I was brought to their small room, and since they both worked hard and a lot, I was left to be attended by a young homeless Jewish survivor who shared the same room and sang to me the Yiddish lullabies. A year before, my father had published a ballade on the massacre of the Jews in his native Utena and at the moment of my birth was suffering the consequences due to Stalin's sudden anti-Semitic altercation. Later, I experienced the respect and thankfulness from Litvaks for this step of my father. . . . My Grandfather Povilas [1890–1964] was mobilized into the Russian army at the beginning of the World War One, and after the revolution fought against the Bolsheviks in the Kolchak army in Siberia. He told sometimes about the disgusting experiences of the Cossacks' pogroms and about his attempts to prevent them. He married there my grandmother, Mariya Zarikhina [1900–1995], a native Siberian, and later returned with her to Independent Lithuania. As an expert of communications, he was appointed to establish the post offices in several shtetls and later told me how positive, cooperative, and enthusiastic were the local Jewish communities towards his activities. The final post office he established was in Utena, where he settled for the rest of his life. He recalled their small but steady Saturday preference community—Grandfather, a postal chief, a doctor, a lawyer, and a local rabbi Knipovith who was the last one to join the company after sunset. . . . We were frequently visiting the flourishing cuttings in the Rashe Forest nearby Utena. I was not allowed to take a single one of the enormously monster wild strawberries. "Let them belong to the rabbi," I was told. And they explained all that had happened.

M. S.: Did your mother's connection with film and theatre have anything to do with your choice to use film as your vehicle for transmitting your singular quest and journey into dangerous territory? With film, one is far more exposed than, say, in the writing of a book.

S. B.: After spending the days watching the rehearsals of my mother and my colleagues, I dreamed of becoming a theatre director. One summer evening walking with my mother along the seashore, I confessed to her my dream. "Turn back and see what remains after our traces," Mother said. Our traces were washed away immediately. "Theatre is the same." This is how I came to the choice of film. Film made me feel safe against the annihilation of memory by time. At the beginning, I still dreamed about fiction—and still remain dreaming—though later was obsessed by documenting of the passing by memory. In contrast to textual documenting, I am obsessed by the possibilities of the audiovisual documentary.

M. S.: If you had all the time, energy and resources to do anything that you wished, what might that project/activity, life work be?

S. B.: "Don't Touch These Strawberries"—an autobiographical documentary about a Lithuanian boy who experienced an atmosphere of the post-Holocaust shtetl, and then devoted himself professionally as a filmmaker to scan the murderers, survivors, and bystanders to make his movies—confessions and to create his Independent Holocaust Archive in Lithuania;

"Meine Vilne"—a personal, concluding documentary by a Lithuanian filmmaker who once recognized his native town as a capital of the Litvak culture and later became its Atlantis—integrating the interviews of those Vilna Litvaks who have passed away;

"Lost in the Sahara"—a documentary musical about the fate of a genius Litvak poetess Matilda Olkinaitė who perished during the Holocaust;

To choose someone who could take upon himself a responsibility towards the collections of my Independent Holocaust Research Archives in Lithuania [videos, documents, photos, testimonies, DB]—to prevent these from going "in five lorries to a dumpimg ground."

M. S.: Are there certain of your films that you feel most strongly about?

S. B.: Sure, Myra! These:

1. "Farewell, Yerushalayim de Lita!";
2. "Unwritten Judel's Diary";
3. "End of the Road";
4. "When Yiddish Was Spoken around Yourbourk";
5. "When Yiddish Was Spoken around Yanishek";
6. "Care";
7. "Lovely Faces of the Murderers."

M. S.: What are you currently working on?

S. B.: "The Petrified Time" [with Sergey Kanovitch/Shadove Jewish Memorial fund]—a unique creative documentary movie on the contemporary confrontation of the Lithuanian and the Jewish views toward Jewish life and its annihilation in a single Litvak shtetl—Shadove.

2

It is not exactly clear how Regina Kopilevich entered my life. As mentioned earlier, when I first came to Lithuania in 1993, I knew no one. If I had thought out more carefully my purpose, I might have postponed the journey for another ten years. Fortunately, I didn't. But after several tries to find a guide without success, in terms of my efforts to discover and visit the towns where my forebears once lived, I had no idea what my next steps might be. The guides I talked to seemed to have little interest in my particular explorations, and spoke mostly Russian, to which I had no access. Language would be a seriously important issue. People in Lithuania spoke Lithuanian, Russian, Polish, German; some few spoke Yiddish, some Hebrew. My Greek and Spanish and English, limited Yiddish and Hebrew, some German, would not be of much help. After several phone conversations with various guides, I took a break.

And then the phone rang. It was Regina. "I am interested in what you are. I will be there in the morning!" Since I had come this far, I had little to lose. I would take my chances. And sure enough, when the next day dawned, Regina was there. A lovely, spirited twenty-nine-year-old greeted me. She had somehow arranged to take me to what would later turn out to be a town of considerable relevance—Kėdainiai—a place where many of my family had once lived. But it was not something I knew at the time. In addition, she had arranged for a survivor of that town, Yudel Ronder, to walk with us and to teach us about life there before the war. For close to twenty-five years, I learned about Lithuania through Regina's eyes and generosity. Whether it was through her location of archival documents of important relevance and prior to digitalization, or her immense gift where we had only to walk into the main road of a village to begin a conversation with the older people of these places who spoke readily to us, or her uncanny sense of what would be meaningful to this stranger, I will always be grateful to her. Her generosity, her ability to move through multiple languages with ease, to sustain the interest of those with whom we spoke, all contributed to the deeply resonant experiences we had. I am not alone in feeling this. Many with whom she has worked and guided share my sense of her. I have not said anything here about being taken into her own life, her sister Dina, her mother, her son Michael who sometimes as a child translated when the going was difficult, meals in their home with others whom she wanted me to know. It has been my great good fortune to know Regina Kopilevich.

WHO ARE OUR TEACHERS? 161

Regina Kopilevich Interview

MYRA SKLAREW: Where and when were you born? Siblings? Parents? Grandparents?

REGINA KOPILEVICH: I was born in Grodno, Belarus [approximately 19 miles from Lithuania]. I spent three days with my mom in the hospital there because the hospital in Druskininkai where we lived was closed. My mom, a medical nurse, worked in the lab of that hospital. My dad was born in Saint Petersburg, graduated medical school there and trained in gastroenterology. He came to Druskininkai for a vacation after medical school and was offered a job there, which is where he met my mother.

My father's parents were born in St. Petersburg; my mother's parents in Druskininkai. Our families were geographically and ethnically quite different. It was very unusual in the nineteen sixties for two people from such divergent backgrounds to marry. My sister Dina was born in nineteen sixty-three; I was born a year later in nineteen sixty-four.

M. S.: How did your parents' very different heritages affect your curiosity to know as much as possible about the history and culture in which you grew up? Did they speak openly to you about their backgrounds and about events in Lithuania where often silence was safer, particularly during the Soviet occupation of Lithuania where at least one generation grew up without knowing much of the contemporary history of the country?

R. K.: They did not speak openly about events. My mom not at all. But my dad always listened to the radio. Though broadcasts were jammed in large cities, in small towns you could listen. I grew up listening to the radio. When not listening for several days, I kept wondering about what's happening in the world. Even to this day I want to know what's happening in the world. My parents never spoke politics. My dad wanted the family to make aliyah, to immigrate, either to Israel or the United States. Despite having earlier been part of the Communist Party, he took an anti-Soviet position and eventually left the Communist Party. He was ill for four years before his early death in nineteen eighty-two at age fifty.

M. S.: How much were you aware of during your early years before the end of the Soviet occupation? How did this affect your choice of study? And your very important work in guiding visitors to Lithuania and providing archival materials for those from all over the world?

R. K.: I decided to study physics at Vilnius University. I knew two languages growing up, Russian and Lithuanian. There were also many Poles and in the school books, magazines, translations with materials/subjects closer to the West. I remember reading detective stories in Polish which provided a window into the West. In nineteen ninety-nine, I went to study in Israel.

Emanuel Zingeris, during the time of Perestroika became part of the Sajūdis which led to the eventual independence of Lithuania. Zingeris served several terms as a member of the Seimas, the Lithuanian Parliament, the only Jew to have done so.

People were attracted to the small towns and villages in Lithuania, to the natural beauty of the country. During the Soviet occupation, people who lost their relatives were prohibited from going to the killing places. The first visitor finally allowed to do so was Abe Resnick who attended the Real Gymnasium in his youth in Kaunas. His family was waiting for him to come home from his school prom and were killed. He escaped to Mexico and eventually to the U.S. where he later became chairman of the board of directors of the United States Holocaust Memorial Museum.

M. S.: I have experienced your fearlessness and genuine interest as you approach new towns, engaging very rapidly with local townspeople, conveying warmth, conversing in multiple languages—Polish, Russian, Lithuanian, German, Yiddish, Hebrew, so that fairly quickly you and those whom you bring with you are conversing with local townspeople who are willing to share their memories of wartime experiences and various occupations of Lithuania. These have been some of the most essential and deep and lasting experiences of my entire life. Can you say a little about how you are able to do this?

R. K.: It is not difficult, but enjoyable, interesting for us. I like Belarus where time is not moving forward. It is like coming back to your childhood. The statue of Lenin is still there, now moved a little bit away, no longer central. People are kind and hospitable. People are more open. Strange fusion of private and political life. I like to communicate with others; it is natural to talk with elderly folks. My Hebrew teacher was Leah Levitt. Exposed to Polish and understood it.

We were able to use the archives as early as nineteen ninety-two, documents of the daily life of the Ghetto, the Ghetto Police records in Yiddish and Lithuanian. In Vilnius, I met with teacher Esther Efros. Schwaba Gymnasium graduate, sister of Efros, a heart surgeon. [There is a new book out on Lithuanian Jewish doctors.]

M. S.: If you had all the time you needed, what would you most wish to do?

R. K.: I would like to read Yiddish and play the piano! In this society, in Vilnius, music plays such a large part of our lives. Opera, the philharmonic, from the age of five, amazing dancers. I was never able to stay still and studied ballet from age five to eight, and was accepted into the school of ballet in Vilnius. But as it required that one must go away from home and live in a dormitory with others, I was not permitted to go. Music stays forever. Amazing standard of music here. The great Lithuanian artist Čiurlionis was both an artist and a composer. He was unique and important. Vytautas Landsbergis wrote a book about Čiurlionis.

M. S.: What has changed over the years that affects your guiding experiences?

R. K.: In helping people find their family histories, the archives is making amazing progress in digitalizing its records. This work gave me the knowledge that saddened me. Early on, I was looking at the world through rose-colored glasses. Now I know that life is not a picnic, that it is sadder.

I have met such fascinating people. For example, in recent times, Professor Georg Klein who discovered the connection between the Epstein-Barr virus and lymphomas and other cancers, and author of *The Atheist and the Holy City, Pieta,* and *Live Now.*

3

I met Rachel Kostanian early in my days in Vilnius, in a small wooden museum called the "Green House" on Pamenkalnio Street. You had to approach the Vilna Gaon Jewish State Museum by ascending a stone stairway to an imposing building set far back from the street, then veering to your right, past houses and parked cars, and up a narrow street to ascend its wooden staircase. To the right, in a small garden there, as you ascended, you would find a beautiful memorial to the Japanese Consul responsible for saving the lives of more than six thousand Jewish people, Chiune Sugihara. At that time, there was no other museum commemorating the Holocaust.

When I visited the museum, I always tried to help if there was a need, whether in editing manuscripts or arranging for translations once I returned to the United States, or wherever I might be needed. One such document of considerable importance was Rachel Kostanian's *Spiritual*

Rachel Kostanian

Resistance in the Vilna Ghetto. Hirsh Dovid Katz wrote, in his excellent review of the book for the *Yiddish Forward* in 2002:

> The author is the well-known deputy director of the Jewish Museum there, Rokhl Kastanian-Danzig.[1] She herself was born in Shavl in the "Kovno Lita" of World War II. She was a child when the war broke out and she managed to escape to Russia, to Gorky, with her mother. The Germans shot her father during the first days of the war. After taking a group of escapees to Dvinsk, he returned to Shavl in order to rescue others. The majority of her family perished. This said, the author is certainly knowledgeable when it comes to the Khurban.

> During the years of Soviet rule, she received a higher education and worked in a completely different field. She is one of the few experts here in today's Lithuania who, with boundless energy and devotion, has managed in the post-Soviet years to educate herself to the point where she is a very serious and knowledgeable scholar and researcher who knows languages, "swallows" books, and is constantly learning more with the energy of a young student who devotes herself body and soul to her chosen subject. Without exaggeration: thousands of Jews from throughout the world who have visited Vilna in recent years come away with amazement at this outstanding woman who built the Khurban Museum in Vilna.[2]

Rachel Kostanian demonstrates in this work the power of cultural resistance under the most dire circumstances. It is stunning to imagine the institutions created during this time as well as the examples of teachers and scholars for those in the Ghetto despite the fact that so many had been killed by 1941.

> As the creator of this system of cultural opposition, she credits, rightfully, the great Yiddish philologue, cultural historian, translator and editor, Zelig Hirsh Kalmonovitch (1885–1944). Kalmonavitch's diary of the ghetto, in Hebrew, was published by his son, the beloved scholar Dr. Shalom Luria, long may he live.
>
> Zelig Hirsh Kalmonovitch was amongst the few educated ones in the ghetto who were deeply involved both in Hebrew and Yiddish; both in the ancient Hebrew and Yiddish civilization, as well as in the modern forms of Jewish culture.[3]

Some of the institutions and activities in the Ghetto included a section for children's education (approximately 1,300 students); six educational institutions (approximately sixty students, with printed diplomas in Yiddish); a music school; a reading room supervised by the beloved librarian and teacher, Chaikl Lunsky (as many as two hundred readers every day); the "Mfitzai Haskala" library (total number of books borrowed reached

100,000); the Farein of writers and artists, with the participation of Zelig Hirsh Kalmonovitch, Herman Kruk, and Avraham Sutzkever; concerts and theater; pages devoted to the traditional religious Yiddish institutions.

It is important to speak here of Rūta Puišytė who worked in the museum and is currently assistant director of the Vilnius Yiddish Institute at Vilnius University. Her bachelor's thesis at Vilnius University, *Holocaust in Jurbarkas: The Mass Extermination of Jews of Jurbarkas in the Provinces of Lithuania during the German Nazi Occupation*,[4] completed in 1997, is a courageous work that names the victims, the executioners, and those righteous Lithuanians who saved Jews, and provides a strong sense of Jewish life before the Holocaust.

During Rūta Puišytė's time at the museum, a major contribution was working with the young people who came from Austria to serve their military time as community service, called Gedenkdienst (Memorial Service). During the years immediately following the end of the Soviet occupation, the museum had only rare visits from local schools and from local non-Jews. A decision to bring the Anne Frank exhibition from Amsterdam to the museum, and to travel with it through the ten main cities of Lithuania, brought audiences of more than ten thousand visitors. The young Austrian volunteers. with the help of Rūta Puišytė. created animated seminars in schools.[5]

On the tenth anniversary of the Gedenkdienst in Lithuania, a celebration honoring the young people who had participated took place, including guests from Austria, the Austrian ambassador Schwarzinger, the young volunteers, colleagues, and staff. On this occasion, Rachel Kostanian spoke:

> Our museum became one of the places where people from all over the world would come to find their roots, their families' stories, to listen to the echoes of the lost world, to stand at the edges of the pits. . . . In the museum a new European mentality was elaborated—a mentality of tolerance, of sharing common values of the civilized world—if I may use this term today. Austrian, Lithuanian, Jewish and Russian cultures and mentalities melted here, I'd say in a new form, where everyone learns from each other, teaches each other.[6]

4

What, in the nature of a person, causes him to risk his own well-being and that of his wife and children to help others? How do we determine the right moment to put aside concern and take action no matter the cost to ourselves? Chiune Sugihara rebelled early, refusing to obey his father's admonition that he study medicine, and pursued study in the Humanities, including proficiency in the Russian language. In 1939, he became vice-consul in Kaunas, Lithuania. In June 1940, the Soviet Union annexed Lithuania. Survival depended upon reaching Japan via the Soviet Union. Jan Zwartendijk, the Dutch Honorary Consul in Lithuania, issued more than 2,300 visas to the island of Curacao. Sugihara bypassed the Japanese requirement that all refugees were allowed only two weeks' stay

Chiune Sugihara

Pen used by Sugihara

Chiune Sugihara Memorial

Simonas Davidavičius

in Japan. During July-August 1940, he issued 2,193 handwritten visas while working eighteen hours per day in the Japanese consulate. And continued to do so until the moment of his departure from Lithuania, filling out visas while on the Kaunas-Berlin train just before it left for Germany, throwing the signed visas through the train window.[7] If you follow his life carefully, you will learn that saving the Jews of Kaunas was not the first of his efforts to read the situation he was in and go against the prescribed course of action in favor of an ethical choice. Nor was his work in Lithuania the last of his independent choices.

Ramūnas Garbaravičius serves as chairman of the Sugihara Foundation and Simonas Davidavičius, the executive director of Sugihara Museum in Kaunas, the Memorial Educational Center of Sugihara. Here, visitors are presented with an up-to-date audiovisual exposition in five historical rooms of the former consulate. The museum has attracted numerous visitors including many from Japan. Simonas Davidavičius completed engineering studies at Kaunas Technological University, and was trained at the Steven Spielberg Visual History Foundation in conducting interviews. In addition to his work for the museum, he is deputy chairman of the Kaunas Jewish Community, responsible for cultural, educational, and financial activities. He has served as chairman of the Kaunas Jewish Community, as a member of the Lithuanian Jewish Community Council, has provided assistance to the United States Holocaust Memorial Museum exhibition, "The Kaunas Ghetto, 1941–1944," and served as interviewer for the Steven Spielberg Visual History Foundation: "Survivors of the Shoah." His travels and presentations have taken him to Japan, Glasgow, Scotland, Sweden, Kaliningrad, and other places. He has served for many years as a guide and archivist for visitors to Lithuania, and I shall always be grateful for his friendship, wisdom, and kindness in helping me to learn about Lithuania and its people.

5

Sara Ginaitė-Rubinson, imprisoned in the Kaunas Ghetto during the war, joined the underground Anti-Fascist Organization resistance movement. After escaping the selection that sent close to ten thousand to their deaths, she determined that she must reject the way the Nazis had arranged her death. "If my fate was to die, I would die on my own terms." On one occasion, she escaped secretly from the Ghetto in order to make contact with other partisans and collect information. She safely crossed the bridge from Villijampolė to Kaunas, met with her contact person, and on her return realized that she was being watched. She proceeded to make her way back across the bridge. The man, though with a limp, followed her and eventually caught up with her. "Nervously, I looked at the Neris River below me. If I'm unable to escape from him, I thought to myself, I'll jump into the river." She managed to return safely to the Ghetto though not without travail. Of that time and experience, she writes: "The memory of running across the bridge, of wanting to jump into the river continued to haunt me. To this day, I can't erase this scene from my memory. I still can't cross a bridge alone, afraid that I'll get the urge to jump into the water."[8] Though the cause of the trauma no longer exists, and the author of these words knows this on a cognitive level, the power of the emotional memory is still operative.

David Wolpe, who survived the Kaunas Ghetto in Lithuania and Dachau Concentration Camp, settled in Johannesburg, South Africa, in the 1950s. He is married with two children and a third on the way. He is eking out a poor living working partly in his brother's factory and doing editing for writers. A visitor has come, courtesy of the Culture Federation of South Africa, from Israel. The guest remarks on the horrendous South African heat of midsummer. "It's a real furnace, but it's nothing like our *khamsin*. You probably remember." He refers to the period of the hot wind in Israel when it is difficult to breathe. And he asks David Wolpe how long it has been since he lived in Israel. "An historical eternity of only two decades," David replies. And then, "Come!" David wished to close off this conversation as quickly as possible, to prevent memory from intruding. Had he not been arrested during a protest march in then-Palestine and deported, he would not have returned to Lithuania in time for the Holocaust. As David describes opening the door of the small veranda of their house to the street, it is as if the door to memory, firmly shut, is inadvertently beginning to open. Before he could prevent it, his guest had climbed over a low fence and seated himself on the cement edge of the road with his feet resting in the culvert. David did likewise, and just as he put his foot down, his "memory brought to the surface . . . the sun-filled summer days in nineteen forty-one. I walk along at the edge of the road, according to the strict Nazi regulation, and overhead the sun shines and guards my steps, as though the whole world would be one shining eye. I walk. Fresh blood-streaks lead to my house. The giant sun-eye gets swollen, like an infected poisonous wound. I pray to heaven to spit it out so that it will explode. And to this day I go and go in those Kovno culverts. And I will always go there, always." His guest misinterprets his sudden silence. And David attempts to explain what has just happened. His guest urges him not to speak of this nor write about it. Best to be quiet, he is urged.⁹

What is striking here in this hallucinatory image of the sun—the source of light and warmth—as an infected wound, is the way in which the body's memory, the placing of the foot down at the side of the road in the culvert, brings forth there in the midst of a domestic ordinary day, the powerful alteration and distortion of the natural world. And the projection of inner fear onto the very guardian of life, the sun. And without the volition of the owner of this memory.

In the case of Ephraim Sten, his daughter Hagit tells us that though we might feel that her father has come to some catharsis, in truth, he did not. "Over the years Father always stressed his reservation about the term attached to him and others as Holocaust survivors [*nitzolim* in Hebrew]. He said there were/are no survivors—in Hebrew the word comes from the root "to save/rescue"—only remnants remain [*s'ridim* in Hebrew]. We were brought up to believe that one couldn't become whole after such an experience . . . this was emphasized . . . one cannot be rescued."¹⁰ In the pages of the journal of Ephraim Sten, *1111 Days in my Life Plus 4*, the adult man meets once more the boy he had been during World War II. At times there is an infinite distance between the boy and the man. At times they are side by side. At times they cross over into one another. And at times, they exchange places.

Ephraim's son Oded writes that "one of the main (if not the most important) issues in the diary is father's gratitude to the saviours. The fact that the diary and the book teach us that at the side of the terrible inhumane acts, there were those who did not lose their humanity and values." Ephraim Sten had the opportunity to see again one of those who saved him, Hryc Tyz. "You are my relatives," Hryc told him. "The Jews I had saved scattered all over the world. . . . I didn't believe I'd be lucky to yet see somebody from my family." Sten never forgot those who had saved his life at great risk to their own, their families, their communities, helping them over all the years that remained to him. In his journal, the boy who suffered confinement and lack of choice and daily mortal threat at a time when youngsters are keenest to explore the world, and the man he became, though never fully integrated, stand together in the exercise of freedom over the voices, faces, images of their shared past.

Chapter X

And So I Lived On

So I lived on, never separating myself from the destroyed ones, not when I was working, resting, or even sleeping. Whomever I met I would ask what they had seen. I would note everything, write it down and think what more I could do.

—Rivka Lozansky-Bogomolnaya,
Wartime Experiences in Lithuania

1

So begins the concluding chapter of Riva Lozansky-Bogomolnaya's testimony, *Wartime Experiences in Lithuania*. Born in Butrimanz (Butrimonys), Lithuania, she had witnessed the mass murder of the Jewish men, women, and children of her town and was determined after the war to locate the murderers and bring them to justice. For this, her house was burned down. But no threat was large enough to dissuade her from this mission.

We met on several occasions. One that stands out in memory is a visit with Saulius Beržinis, the filmmaker and her friend, to the hospital where she was a patient. I don't think I've ever seen caring as tender as I saw that day. He opens his briefcase and takes out a brush to gently brush her hair. Then he most carefully washes her face, talking quietly with her, turning her so she will not get bed sores. He unfolds the shirt lying next to her and opens the pocket to take out a small packet with some bills for the doctors and nurses. We add some Litas to it and Saulius pins it back into the pocket. Riva was in a hospital room with five other patients, where care was hard to come by.

Riva Lozansky during war

Riva Lozansky

"From the age of sixteen, I was a member of Gordon, a Zionist organization that provided work for the youth," Riva says. Here, she learned about Palestine, studied Hebrew and Jewish history. When some in her group immigrated to Palestine before the war, she had the opportunity to go but did not want to leave her family. Riva Lozansky describes the makeup of those in Butrimantz (Butrimonys)—Lithuanians, Tatars, and, in nearby villages, Poles. She speaks of Jews having friends of varying nationalities. "In the beginning of the nineteen-thirties, when hooligans from surrounding towns tried to create a pogrom, every person in Butrimantz (Butrimonys) stood up to stop it. . . . The villains were defeated that time. They ran away as far as they could, until the summer of nineteen forty-one . . ."[1]

Riva's father was a lumberjack and knew the forests, and when offered the chance to lead a group through the forests and make their way to Russia, he refused. "Three of my daughters are not with me at this time. I'm not going anywhere without them." They were not afraid of their neighbors as they had not known anti-Semitism previously. After the German invasion, it was Lithuanian activists (members of the LAF, wearing white armbands) who were mobilized by the Germans.

When Riva was hiding in Lithuanian forests, she would go to non-Jewish villagers asking for food, as well as "pencil and paper. In the margins of the scraps of newspaper she'd receive, she kept a diary of her experiences."[2] Not until her eighties did she complete the memoir of her earlier experiences. Unlike many of the few survivors in Lithuania, Riva Lozansky-Bogomolnaja did not leave Lithuania after the war but remained to act as a "one-person memorial committee and vengeance squad," locating the mass graves throughout Lithuania and attempting to bring the murderers to justice.

In 1991, a Polish woman whose father had been killed for hiding Jews mentioned to Riva that two war criminals whom she'd helped send to prison . . . had been officially rehabilitated by the new nationalist government.[3] Though she attempted to have these pardons suspended, providing the names of witnesses, it was not until the *New York Times*, via the help of Efraim Zuroff of the Simon Wiesenthal Center, gave this issue front-page visibility that the rehabilitation scandal became headlines around the world. As a result a commission was established by the Lithuanian and Israeli governments to examine the issue of rehabilitations.

So we come to the fierce life of a woman who, even in her eighties, was a guardian of the truth. Of the two thousand Jewish people of Butrimantz (Butrimonys), ten survived. And through the persistence and determination of one of these—Riva Lozansky-Bogomolnaja—what took place in her country is not buried.

2

Return. When we say this word, for some it invokes a three-part sequence: dispersion, exile, return—as during the Judean dispersion from Jerusalem and the destruction of the temple there in 586 BCE, the exile to Babylonia and Egypt, and the eventual return to Jerusalem. In some cases, according to the Old Testament, there was no return—not to the Garden of Eden, nor for Abraham to his homeland Ur in Mesopotamia, and for others, like Moses, there was permanent exile, only the possibility of looking over to the land of Canaan but never being allowed to return.

So what does the notion of return mean to those few who survived the Holocaust in Lithuania? For many, psychologically, they had never really left Lithuania. Their trauma was a constant, living visage. But there were those who eventually desired to witness again the place of their birth, of their early childhood, when they had lived among those they loved who were missing. Shalom Eilati, in "Back to the River" begins with these lines from Genesis (19:26): "But Lot's wife looked back, and she became a pillar of salt."

> And in the end, did I ever return? As with so many of my friends, I too had deep-seated reasons for rejecting the idea out of hand: the abhorrence, amounting to hatred, of this land of blood, where so many of its citizens had served as enthusiastic hangmen. And whom will you visit there, with all your dear ones absent; your rescuers no longer alive; the ghetto long since destroyed and its land built over again. Will you go to find out who the Lithuanians are who now live in the house you lived in before the war.[4]

Eilati wonders about the purpose of returning to the present "tranquil landscapes . . . like a pastoral blanket" that belies what actually took place there. However, he asks if by confronting the memories might he "diminish their strength." He points out that Lot's wife did look back. Yet he had been commanded by his mother when crossing the river in his childhood not to look back. He obeyed and was saved. It took another fifty-five years before Eilati could actually decide to return to Lithuania.

I am reminded here of the letter Elchanan Elkes—physician and head of the Ältestenrat, the Jewish Council in the Kovno Ghetto—wrote to his son Joel and daughter Sara. It is dated October 19, 1943. The Kovno Ghetto was one of the few where the head of the Council was elected by the community. Dr. Elkes, who believed in the sanctity of life, had no desire to take on this responsibility that involved daily interaction with the Nazis. He saw himself as the physician he was, whose prime purpose had to do with healing, not death. Eventually, at the urging of the community, he agreed to do so.

In his letter, he admonishes his children never to return to Lithuania: "Remember, both of you, what Amalek has done to us. Remember and never forget it all your days; and pass this memory as a sacred testament to future generations."[5] The letter is a farewell to his children. His life ended in Dachau.

Shalom Eilati did return to Lithuania. Twice. "I count the possessions that are left to me: a roofless building in the old quarter, a pile of rubble in back country with shoots of a pear tree sprouting from it, a factory that holds traces of my mother, a stone path that climbs the Green Hill and guards her footsteps, a little open place where the image of my sister is etched, and a patchwork of mass graves in groves saturated with blood." He tells us that he "may not have found an actual home where I belong, but at the least I located my longing for it."[6]

Solly Ganor did return to Lithuania. "The flight from Tel Aviv to Vilnius lasts only four hours, but my memory takes me back more than sixty years when my life was violently disrupted by the Nazi invasion of Lithuania on June 21, 1941. One day I was a happy, spoiled thirteen-year-old boy, and overnight I became a hunted animal who could be sought out and killed by anyone who felt like it." Ganor asks why someone who had suffered such trauma as a child would decide to return after sixty years. "Throughout the flight I was in a panic and if I could have turned the plane around, I would have done it."[7] He didn't know how he would react when he took his first steps on Lithuanian soil, "the soil I swore never to step on as long as I live. Did I expect to be struck down by lightning, or hear a stern voice speaking to me from heaven for breaking my vow?"[8] As he was landing at the Vilnius Airport, Ganor caught a glimpse of the dozens of church steeples and cathedrals and the tower of Gediminas Castle that children before the war had been taught to revere. The family planned a gathering at the gravesite of their cousin, Professor Aleksandras Štromas.

"Full of apprehension, I stepped out to the waiting hall and to my great relief saw among the small crowd waiting there the familiar face of my cousin Irena," Ganor recalls. "She just smiled and gave me a big hug and much of the apprehension dissipated." His cousin, Irena Veisaitė, scholar, human rights advocate, and intellectual, who had been saved by a Lithuanian Christian family, remained in Lithuania after the war where she taught at the University of Vilnius.

Another form of return for Solly Ganor is his belonging to the Association of Survivors of Landsberg/Kaufering (Dachau), which gathers each April to commemorate "our perished brothers and sisters." In a letter, he mentions a Wolpe who was incarcerated with him, quite likely my cousin Leiser or my uncle David, who were in Dachau at that time.

3

Another curious aspect of traumatic memory is the way significant moments in a life seem to be erased. These are not, to our knowledge, traumatic moments but times of reconciliation and comfort.

Edith Lowy describes surviving the war in concentration camps and forced marches, always keeping in mind the image of her father, the deep belief that she will see her father again, if only she can manage to stay alive. She and her father are the only members of the immediate family to survive the war. Of that first meeting between the child and her absent father, she remembers nothing. Throughout her life she has attempted to recall those first precious moments of reunion, but though her memory for multiple details of her experiences seems to her to be completely intact, this memory is a lacuna. Entirely erased. The other strange lapse in memory for her is the name of the friend with whom she went through the entire experience in the concentration camp.[9]

Eta Hecht remembers in great detail the Kinder Aktion where the majority of the children in the Kovno Ghetto were rounded up, dragged from their hiding places, put on lorries and killed at the Ninth Fort, despite the fact that at the time she was four and a half years old. She was one of the very few whose hiding place behind a stairway and under a mattress—to this day she has a fear of suffocation—was not discovered. In a period of a few weeks she was required to learn Lithuanian (her only language at the time was Yiddish), and to relinquish her Jewish identity so that she could be hidden with a family who had agreed to take her in. She was put in a tool sack, carried out of the Ghetto on her mother's back as she went to forced labor, and given—in a prearranged plan—to a woman who would deliver her to the family. At a certain point that family felt it was too dangerous to keep her and she was given to another family out in the countryside. Though she was with that second family for some eighteen months, and though there were other children in that family, she has no recollection of anything that took place during that time. As if in stop-time, what was forgotten is bounded on either side by rich memories with her family earlier, and with the reconciliation with her parents afterward.[10]

Charlotte Noshpitz played an active role in the French Resistance and was not incarcerated, though her mother was taken in the first round-up of foreign nationals on July 16, 1942, and died in Auschwitz, and her brother was killed as well. She describes searching for many years for a memory of the Passover Seder in her family home. Each year, when she attends the Seder at the home of friends, she tries again to recollect even the least detail of the family celebration of Passover, but she cannot.

In the case of two of these, the memories they search for are not traumatic but are of reassuring, comforting times. But they are lost to their owners, somehow no longer available. One could ask: To what are these experiences attached? Does remembering the reunion with a father after great suffering carry with it the danger of remembering the specific suffering as well, though that seems intact in memory? Does remembering a time of comfort, safely in the home, celebrating the passage from slavery to freedom, involve remembering some part of the trauma that is not available to conscious memory? Consider the child handed over first to one family and then to a second, without understanding why she cannot be with her mother and father—with the sense that they are

Charlotte Noshpitz

gone for good, as well as her very identity including her language. It is not difficult to imagine why she may not remember the years when she endured this separation.

4

The poet Osip Mandelstam writes: "All the elegant mirage of Petersburg was merely a dream, a brilliant covering thrown over the abyss, while round about there sprawled the chaos of Judaism—not a motherland, not a house, not a hearth, but precisely a chaos, the unknown womb whence I had issued, which I feared, about which I made vague conjectures and fled, always fled."[11]

Norman Manea speaks of being acutely aware of "the fatigue of belonging," of both "the perils of uprootedness . . . [and] the hazards of rootedness." This conflict forms the central and most troubling theme of his book. Most basically, it underlies Manea's anxious reluctance to belong to the Jewish community. As a boy, he saw in his family "a restricted world, trapped by its own fears and frustrations, a ghetto suffering from the disease of the past." And to explain his lifelong refusal to let himself "be reclaimed by the clan," Manea points to the lessons of the past: "After my juvenile fling with the Communist madness, I had come to hate anything that had to do with 'we,' with collective identity, which seemed to me suspect, an oppressive simplification. I am an embarrassed inhabitant of my own biography."[12]

These struggles about identity remind me of the words of Charlotte Sorkine Noshpitz, a member of the French Resistance during World War II who was responsible for saving the lives of hundreds of children, taking them to the Swiss border where they were brought to safety, and for the lives of adult men who escaped over the Pyrenees Mountains into Spain. She was involved in the liberation of Paris and forged hundreds of false documents. She told me once: "I stopped my friendship with God when I was young, and witnessed the hanging deaths of three men in a truck in Paris during the occupation." Or as Yocheved Inčiūrienė commented, she had recently read the Tanakh and had decided that she did not want to participate in the Jewish religion. "The God that is depicted there is too punitive."

These issues have extreme relevance in the present time where our peoples of this earth are divided and restricted by country of birth, religion, political regime.

5

We must ask where it is we have arrived. What do we know about memory at this point? Can we say with certainty that overwhelming experience is taken in differently than normal experience? And that it is not only encoded differently, but that its retrieval differs as well? That the greatly increased affective energies at the time of the trauma alter the normal experience of memory.

What we've learned from those who have shared their memories is the many varied responses to trauma. Does traumatic experience serve to motivate taking action as Riva Lozansky-Bogomolnaya did or Charlotte Noshpitz did during the French Resistance, or does the power of traumatic memories cause retreat and withdrawal? Some seek solace (or reconciliation or healing) in the act of returning to the place where the trauma occurred, and others find this intolerable. How do we understand why some memories remain intact and others are no longer accessible by normal means? And what are the qualities and meaning of those memories that endure?

We witness the various hypotheses of memory formation. Perhaps the most unusual is that of neurophysiologist Karl Pribram[13] who offers a holographic model for the storage of memories. Pribram's holographic theory of brain/mind is similar to the biological system where every cell contains in its DNA a template of the entire organism. Pribram suggests that we perceive the environment in terms of frequencies of light, sound, vibrations, which are stored as resonant circuits in the nervous system. Conscious processes—memory, perception, imagery, emotion—involve reading out of this complexity through the transformation of the hologram back into patterns of neuronal firing. We are essentially interpreting frequencies.

Perhaps David Wolpe's description of a nightmare illustrates Pribram's theory. As it does teach us about the endurance and the power of trauma. May he, like all who speak here, be our teacher.

> During a restless night, in one of my nightmares I saw my childhood. It was an image suspended on a leafless branch hanging over the grave of the disembodied community of Keidan. How was it that I knew it was me and my own childhood? It was from the vision of a child's withered hand stretched across the strings of a shattered brown fiddle. It belonged to my uncle Chaim Oppenheim.
>
> There was a time when I used to steal into my Bobbe Leah's living room and stare at a black violin case hanging high on a wall. So high that it seemed as if only an angel could ascend to it. One day I found the treasured content resting on a small music table beside the wall. I stroked it, plucked

the strings and drew out a sound. On another occasion, I did the same, causing something to vibrate faintly in my inner being, evoking the sweetness of childhood magic. With that sound in my mind's ear I later fell asleep.

And when my life force bore me across a tiny pile of glowing ash, changing my status from concentration camp victim to survivor, there began the chapters of my blinding nightmares. On a certain night, whilst lying in a hospital bed, I suddenly heard the wail of torn strings. Strenuously, I opened my eyes and saw resting on top of a huge pile of black boxes reaching skywards, the shattered fiddle of my childhood, rocking and weeping.[14]

notes

Notes to Beginnings

1. Anne Truitt speaks about this in her book about her experience as interim director of Yaddo, *Turn: The Journal of an Artist* (New York: Penguin Press, 1987).

2. Michael Steinlauf, *Bondage to the Dead: Poland the Memory of the Holocaust* (Syracuse: Syracuse University Press, 1997).

3. Phillip Hallie, *Lest Innocent Blood Be Shed* (New York: Harper and Row, 1979) and in conversation with Magda Trocme in Washington, D.C., and with former members of the French Resistance.

4. Pranas Matiukas was killed in 1962 by the KGB.

5. Richard Burgin, *Jorge Luis Borges: Conversations* (Jackson: University Press of Mississippi, 1968), 10–11.

6. Ibid., 28.

7. Dominick LaCapra, *Writing History, Writing Trauma* (Baltimore: Johns Hopkins University Press, 2013).

8. Miklos Radnoti, *Clouded Sky* (New York: Sheep Meadow Press, 2003).

9. Dan Pagis, *The Selected Poetry of Dan Pagis* (Berkeley: University of California Press, 1996), 39.

10. Robert Alter, "Introduction," in Dan Pagis, *Points of Departure*, trans. Stephen Mitchell (Philadelphia: Jewish Publication Society of America, 1982).

11. Pagis, *The Selected Poetry*.

12. Alter, in Pagis, *Points of Departure*.

13. Paul Celan, Acceptance Speech, Bremen Prize for German Literature, 1958.

14. Michael Rothberg, *Traumatic Realism: The Demands of Holocaust Representation* (Minneapolis: University of Minnesota Press, 2000), 41.

15. Elie Wiesel, *The Gates of the Forest* (New York: Schocken, 1995).

16. Jean Amery, *At the Mind's Limits: Contemplations by a Survivor on Auschwitz and its Realities* (Bloomington: Indiana University Press, 2009).

17. Peter Kenez, *Varieties of Fear: Growing Up Jewish under Nazism and Communism* (Bloomington, IN: iUniverse, 2001).

18. Wiesel, *The Gates of the Forest*.

19. In conversation with the author.

20. Pliny the Younger, *The Epistles of Pliny the Younger* (Edinburgh: A. Donaldson and J. Reis, 1762).

21. Radnoti, *Clouded Sky*.

22. Shlomo Breznitz, *Memory Fields* (New York: Doubleday, 1993).

23. In conversation with the author.

24. G. E. Schafft and William H. Kincade, "Holes in Their Histories: Public History and Public Policy," *International Studies Notes* 18, no. 2 (Spring 1983): 6–14.

25. Ibid.

26. Primo Levi, "The Memory of the Offense," in *The Drowned and the Saved* (New York: Summit Books, 1988).

27. Charlotte Delbo, *Days and Memory*, trans. Rosette Lamont (Evanston, IL: Marlboro Press, 2001).

28. Amery, *At the Mind's Limits*.

29. Aharon Appelfeld. *The Story of a Life* (New York: Schocken Books, 2004), 90.

Chapter I. In the Ponar Forest

1. Kazimierz Sakowicz, *Ponary Diary, 1941–1943: A Bystander's Account of a Mass Murder* (New Haven: Yale University Press, 2005), 12; Joseph Levinson, ed., *The Shoah in Lithuania* (Vilnius, Lithuania: The Vilna Gaon Jewish State Museum/VAGA Publishers, 2006).

2. Abba Kovner, *A Canopy in the Desert: Selected Poems* (Pittsburgh: University of Pittsburgh Press, 1973).

3. Excerpt from "My Mother's Story," in Stanley Kunitz, *Next to Last Things: New Poems and Essays* (New York: Atlantic Monthly Press, 1985), 75–79.

4. Interview with author for United States Holocaust Memorial Museum.

5. Conversation with the author.

6. Kazimierz Sakowicz, *Ponary Diary, 1941–1943, A Bystander's Account of a Mass Murder* (New Haven: Yale University Press, 2005), 2–3.

7. Liudas Truska. *The Upsurge of Antisemitism in Lithuania in the Years of the Soviet Occupation (1940–1941)* (Vilnius: 2001), 23.

8. Krystyna Chiger. *The Girl in the Green Sweater* (New York: St. Martin's Press, 2008), 2.

Chapter II. Versions

1. Saulius Sužiedėlis, "The Burden of 1941," *Lituanus* 47, no. 4 (Winter 2001).

2. Author interview with witness. Vandžiogala, Lithuania, 1994.

3. Joseph Levinson, ed., *The Shoah (Holocaust) in Lithuania* (Vilnius: The Vilna Gaon Jewish State Museum/VAGA Publishers, 2006), 491.

4. Thomas Burgenthal, interview, United States Holocaust Memorial Museum, Washington, DC.

5. Robert Kraft, *Memory Perceived: Recalling the Holocaust* (Westport, CT: Praeger, 2002).

6. *Homefront: Stories of America at War*, a student-created documentary. Produced by Rick Rockwell. American University School of Communications, 2007.

7. *The Tree That Remembers*, directed by Masoud Raouf (Chicago: Olive Films, 2007), DVD.

8. Chiger, *The Girl in the Green Sweater*, 249.

Chapter III. Out of Sight

1. *Judaism*, 110.

2. Rabbi Ephraim Oshry. *The Annihilation of Lithuanian Jewry* (New York: Judaica Press, 1995).

3. Ibid., 135.

4. Ephraim F. Sten. *1111 Days in My Life Plus Four* (Takoma Park: Dryad Press, 2006), 138.

5. Ibid.

6. Shira Nayman, *Awake in the Dark* (New York: Simon and Schuster, 2006).

7. Ibid.

8. Ibid.

9. Ibid.

Chapter IV. Leiser's Song

1. Ada Wolpe. Letter to the author.
2. We learn only now that David Wolpe carefully preserved Leiser's letters, and after David's death when his children gave his papers to archives, it became clear that these remarkable letters, written just after the war, in beautiful Yiddish, do in fact exist.
3. Oshry, *The Annihilation of Lithuanian Jewry*; and Rabbi Ephraim Oshry, *Responsa from the Holocaust* (New York: The Judaica Press, 1989).
4. There is no consensus thus far about what happened to the children who were taken from the Kovno Ghetto during the two-day Children's Action when German troops and Ukrainian auxilliaries rounded up those who remained. Shalom Eilati, a child survivor in hiding, recalls hearing cursing in German and Ukrainian as children are pulled crying from their mothers and speaks of buses for transport. "So it seems that the Aktion against children—the Kinder Aktion—encoded and prefigured the manner of the Ghetto's destruction," he writes in *Crossing the River* (University of Alabama Press, 2008, 130). According to Leib Garfunkel, the vice-chairman of the Jewish Council of the Kovno Ghetto, one thousand children and elders were taken on March 27, 1944, on buses with windows covered and driven in the direction of the city of Kovno, three hundred on the next day. According to researchers at the USHMM, it is still unclear the manner in which the children were killed. Other accounts state that the children were taken in trucks/lorries to the Ninth Fort and killed.
5. Robert L. Hilliard, *Surviving the Americans: The Continued Struggle for the Jews after Liberation* (New York: Seven Stories Press, 1996).
6. Solly Ganor, *Light One Candle: A Survivor's Tale from Lithuania to Jerusalem* (New York: Kodansha America, 1995).
7. Rainer Maria Rilke, "Autumn," in *The Poetry of Rainer Maria Rilke*, trans. M. D. Herter Norton (New York: W.W. Norton, 1962), 74–75.

Chapter V. Lietūkis Garage Massacre

1. Vera Silkinaitė, interview by Saulius Beržinis, trans. Anna Zlotak (Vilnius: Lithuania Documentation Project, 1998, 2000–01), USHMM: RG-50.473.003. The director of the Department of Oral History was Joan Ringelheim, and Nathan Beyrak was project director. This information is corroborated and added to by survivor Yocheved Inčiūrienė, friend of Vera Silkinaitė.
2. Irena Čarževskienė, interview (Vilnius: Lithuania Documentation Project, 1998, 2000–01), USHMM: RG-50.473.015. Čarževskienė was a witness to the Lietūkis garage pogrom, born March 17, 1928, in Kaunas, Lithuania.

3. Jasiūnas Rimgaudas, interview (Vilnius: Lithuania Documentation Project, 1998, 2000–01), USHMM: RG-50.473.017. Rimgaudas was born January 30, 1931, in Kaunas, Lithuania.

4. From the manuscript, Dimitri Gelpernas's *Kovno Ghetto Diary*; and later, Dimitri Gelpernas and Meir Yelin, *Partisans of Kovno Ghetto*, trans. Chaim Bargman, from original Yiddish into Russian, Kaunas 1994. The manuscript was given to Robin O'Neil by Bargman and Gelpernas in Vilnius in 1995, and O'Neil translated the document from Russian into English in 1996.

5. William W. Mishell, *Kaddish for Kovno: Life and Death in a Lithuanian Ghetto 1941–1945* (Chicago: Chicago Review Press, 1988), 25. Told by Dr. Max Solc, brother-in-law of Mishell; Daniel Bar-On, "The Bystander in Relation to the Victim and the Perpetrator: Today and During the Holocaust," *Social Justice Research* 14, no. 2 (June 2001): 125–48.

Chapter VI. Return

1. Told to author.
2. Rachel Langosch, "Lithuania: A Place to Remember; A Place to Forget" (student paper, Bard College, 2002).
3. Ibid.
4. Solly Ganor. Interview by Rachel Langosch, 2002.
5. Rachel Langosch, "Lithuania: A Place to Remember; A Place to Forget."

Chapter VII. Trauma Made Manifest

1. Sam Schalkowsky, *The Clandestine History of the Kovno Ghetto Police* (Bloomington: Indiana University Press, 2014).

2. Ibid., xi.

3. Zev Birger, *No Time for Patience: My Road from Kaunas to Jerusalem* (New York: HarperCollins, 1999).

4. His uncle, David Wolpe, writes that in the middle of the night on June 23, 1941, young bands of Lithuanian youth calling themselves "partisans"—armed and drunk, and before the Nazis established themselves in the city of Kovno (Kaunas)—tore into the courtyard of Laisvės Alėja where his brother and nephew lived. They gathered sixty men and boys in a basement and shot everyone, including thirteen-year-old Leiser (actually sixteen years old). All were killed except for Leiser, who pretended to be dead and later went for help. He had been shot but survived. The doctor who stitched up his wounds was astonished. Leiser said he raised his hand to protect his heart, and a pen in his

pocket saved him; in David E. Wolpe, "*Ich un Main Welt (I and My World)*" (Johannesburg-Jerusalem: Zur-Ot, 1997), 231.

5. Conversation with the author.
6. Shalom Eilati, *Crossing the River*, 46.
7. Ibid.
8. Ibid.
9. Ibid.
10. Ibid., 132.
11. Ibid. Julija Grincevičienė. Eilati was saved by others as well, whom he later nominated to be honored at Yad Vashem. The willingness of some people to hide Jews, putting their families and communities in mortal danger, is a vital part of this period and deserves its own place in this history.
12. Ibid., ix, x.
13. Eilati, *Crossing the River*, 32–33. This citation is from the unpublished manuscript, which was sent to me by the author as it was being prepared for publication.
14. Myra Sklarew, letter to Norton.
15. Judith Lewis Herman. *Trauma and Recovery* (New York: Basic Books, 1997), 34–35.
16. Antonio R. Damasio, "An Interview with Antonio R. Damasio," interview by Conor Liston, *The Harvard Brain* 8 (2001): 2.
17. Jorge Luis Borges, *Labyrinths* (New York: New Directions, 1964), 54–55.
18. Regina Pally, *The Mind-Brain Relationship* (Abingdon: Routledge, 2000), 8–9.
19. i.e., Dr. C. on the Garage Massacre.
20. Joseph LeDoux, *The Emotional Brain: The Mysterious Underpinnings of Emotional Life* (New York: Simon and Schuster, 1996), 112.
21. Bessel A. van der Kolk, Alexander C. McFarlane, and Lars Weisaeth, *Traumatic Stress: The Effects of Overwhelming Experience on Mind, Body, and Society* (New York/London: The Guilford Press, 1996), 216–17.
22. Joseph LeDoux. "Parallel Memories: Putting Emotions Back into the Brain: A Talk with Joseph LeDoux," *Edge*, February 17, 1997, https://www.edge.org/conversation/joseph_ledoux-parallel-memories-putting-emotions-back-into-the-brain.
23. Ibid.
24. Scott P. Edwards, "The Amygdala: The Body's Alarm Circuit," *Brain Work: The Neuroscience Newsletter* 15, no. 3 (2005).
25. Richard Restak, "'Rapid Response,' review of *The Emotional Brain: The Mysterious Underpinnings of Emotional Life*, by Joseph LeDoux," *New York*

Times Book Review, Dec. 1, 1996, https://www.nytimes.com/1996/12/01/books/rapid-response.html.

26. Author interview with Keren Kristin, USHMM, May 18, 1995.

27. Shalom Eilati, *Crossing the River*. English translation in manuscript, 71.

28. Ibid., 75.

Chapter VIII. Rescue

1. Interview with S. B.

2. Julija Šukys, *And I Burned with Shame: The Testimony of Ona Šimaitė, Righteous Among the Nations, A Letter to Isaac Nachman Steinberg (Search and Research, Band 10)* (Göttingen: Wallstein Verlag GmbH, 2008), 12.

3. Information provided in manuscript form and in conversation with Dr. Petras Baublys's colleague, Dr. Elena Miknevičienė, and with visits to two of the nurses, 1994.

4. Dr. Elena Miknevičienė, unpublished manuscript, 1994.

5. Saulius Beržinis, interview by Bronius Elijošaitis, trans. Alicija Žukauskaitė, summarized by Akvilė Žilionytė.

6. *Hands Bringing Life and Bread: Volume 1* (Vilnius: The Vilna Gaon Jewish State Museum, 1997).

7. J. Čartokaitė-Inčiūrienė, "Surviving Through German Occupation (Memories)," *Baltos Lankos* 5 (1995).

8. Yocheved Inčiūrienė, interview by Myra Sklarew, Kaunas, Lithuania, 1996.

9. Yocheved Inčiūrienė, "To Survive Under the German Ocupation in Lithuania," *Baltos Lantos* 5.

10. Ibid. Yocheved Inčiūrienė told me that it was finally a shoemaker's wife from Kaunas who recognized her that forced her to leave the Saunoris farm and go into hiding with the help of Jurgis Inčiūra and his mother.

11. Jean Saunoris, letter to Yad Vashem, Montreal, December 24, 1993.

12. On August 29, 2016, on the seventy-fifth anniversary of the killing of the Jews of Molėtai, a march of the living expected to include some three hundred people turned out to be more than three thousand, including priests, Franciscan monks, military, students, teachers, engineers, young and old, as well as the president of Lithuania, Dalia Gribauskaitė, ambassadors, and Vytautas Landsbergis (first president of post-Soviet Lithuania) and his wife. Many non-Jews attached Jewish stars to their clothing. The prevailing majority of the marchers were non-Jews.

Chapter IX. Who Are Our Teachers?

1. In 2001, the Center for Tolerance opened, providing numerous exhibitions, concerts, and symposia. The Jewish Community Building honors those who rescued Jews from the Nazis.

2. Dovid Katz, "A New Book about the Cultural Life in the Vilna Ghetto," review of *Spiritual Resistance in the Vilna Ghetto*, by Rachel Kostanian, *The Yiddish Forward*, August 16, 2002 (translated by Miriam Dashkin Beckerman, Canada).

3. Ibid.

4. Rūta Puišytė, "Holocaust in Jurbarkas: The Mass Extermination of Jews in Jurbarkas in the Provinces of Lithuania during the German Nazi Occupation" (BA thesis, Vilnius University, 1997), www.shtetlinks.jewishgen.org/yurburg/bathesis.html.

5. *Austria's Unique Approach to Cooperation in Holocaust Research and Education: Gedenkdienst in Vilnius 1995–2008* (Vilnius: Žara Publishers, 2008), 14–15.

6. Ibid., 15–16.

7. "Sugihara House: Between the Past and the Present" (Museum Document, Sugihara House, Kaunas, Lithuania).

8. Sara Ginaitė-Rubinson, *Resistance and Survival: The Jewish Community in Kaunas 1941–1945* (Oakville, Ontario: Mosaic Press, 2005), 115. And from a talk given by Sara Ginaitė-Rubinson, North York, Canada, 2006.

9. David E. Wolpe, *Ich un Main Welt (I and My World)*, manuscript, 119 (translated from Yiddish by Miriam Dashkin Beckerman).

10. In conversation with the author.

Chapter X. And So I Lived On

1. Olga Zabludoff and Lily Poritz Miller, eds., *If I Forget Thee . . . The Destruction of the Shtetl Butrimantz* (Washington, DC: Remembrance Books, 1998), 20–21.

2. Yossi Klein Halevi, "Murderers, She Wrote," *The Jerusalem Report*, November 14, 1996, 32.

3. Ibid.

4. Shalom Eilati, *Back to the River*, manuscript, 4.

5. Joel Elkes. *Dr. Elkhanan Elkes of the Kovno Ghetto: A Son's Memoir* (Brewster, MA: Paraclete Press, 1999), 92.

6. Shalom Eilati, *Back to the River*, manuscript, 23.

7. "Returning Home to Lithuania," an article sent to me in a letter from Solly Ganor on November 5, 2003.

8. Ibid.

9. In conversation with the author.

10. Ibid.

11. Osip Mandelstam, *The Noise of Time*, in Osip Mandelstam, *Selected Poems*, trans. Clarence Brown and W. S. Merwin (New York: Atheneum, 1974), vi.

12. Benjamin Balint, "Capturing the Meanderings of Memory," *Forward*, October 10, 2003; Norman Manea, *The Hooligan's Return: A Memoir* (New York: Farrar, Straus and Giroux, 2003), 13.

13. Dr. Karl Pribram was director of the program at Yale University School of Medicine, Department of Neurophysiology, with whom I worked studying the prefrontal cortex and delayed-response memory in the 1950s.

14. David E. Wolpe, *Ich un Main Welt (I and My World)* (Johannesburg-Jerusalem, 1997), III–IV.

bibliography

Abramovich, Solomon, and Yakov Zilberg, eds. *Smuggled in Potato Sacks: Fifty Stories of the Hidden Children of the Kaunas Ghetto.* London: Vallentine Mitchell, 2011.

Alkon, Daniel L. *Memory's Voice: Deciphering the Mind-Brain Code.* New York: HarperCollins, 1992.

Alter, Robert. "Introduction." In Dan Pagis, *Points of Departure*, translated by Stephen Mitchell. Philadelphia: Jewish Publication Society of America, 1982.

Amery, Jean. *At the Mind's Limits: Contemplations by a Survivor on Auschwitz and its Realities.* Bloomington: Indiana University Press, 2009.

Appelfeld, Aharon. *The Story of a Life.* New York: Schocken Books, 2004.

Austria's Unique Approach to Cooperation in Holocaust Research and Education: Gedenkdienst in Vilnius 1995–2008. Vilnius: Žara, 2008.

Balint, Benjamin. "Capturing the Meanderings of Memory." *Forward*, October 10, 2003.

Baliukevičius, Lionginas. *The Diary of a Partisan: A Year in the Life of the Postwar Lithuanian Resistance Fighter Dzukas.* Vilnius: Genocide and Resistance Centre of Lithuania, 2008.

Bar-On, Dan. *Fear and Hope: Three Generations of the Holocaust.* Cambridge: Harvard University Press, 1995.

Bar-On, Daniel. "The Bystander in Relation to the Victim and the Perpetrator: Today and During the Holocaust." *Social Justice Research* 14, no. 2 (June 2001): 125–48.

Ben-Dor, David. *The Darkest Chapter.* Edinburgh: Canongate, 1996.

Bergmann, Martin S. *In the Shadow of Moloch.* New York: Columbia University Press, 1992.

———, and Milton E. Jucovy. *Generations of the Holocaust.* New York: Basic Books, 1982.

Beržinis, Saulius. Interview with Bronius Elijošaitis. Translated by Alicija Žukauskaitė. Summarized by Akvilė Žilionytė.
Birger, Zev. *No Time for Patience: My Road from Kaunas to Jerusalem.* New York: HarperCollins, 1999.
Bogomolnaya, Rivka Lozansky. *Wartime Experiences in Lithuania.* London: Vallentine Mitchell, 2000.
Borges, Jorge Luis. *Labyrinths.* New York: New Directions, 1964.
Brauns, Jack. *Recollections and Reflections: How I Turned Despair into an Appreciation of Life.* London: Vallentine Mitchell, 2007.
Breznitz, Shlomo. *Memory Fields.* New York: Doubleday, 1993.
Bubnys, Arūnas. *Nazi Resistance Movement in Lithuania: 1941–1944.* Vilnius: Vaga, 2003.
Buckner, R. L., S. E. Peterson, J. G. Ojeman, F. M. Miezin, L. R. Squire, and M. E. Raichle. "Functional Anatomical Studies of Explicit Memory Retrieval Tasks." *Journal of Neuroscience* 15 (1995): 12–29.
Burgenthal, Thomas. Interview, United States Holocaust Memorial Museum, Washington, DC.
Burgin, Richard. *Jorge Luis Borges: Conversations.* Jackson: University Press of Mississippi, 1968.
Čartokaitė-Inčiūrienė, J. "Surviving Through German Occupation (Memories)." *Baltos Lankos* 5 (1995).
Caruth, Cathy. *Unclaimed Experience: Trauma, Narrative, and History.* Baltimore: Johns Hopkins University Press, 1996.
Cassedy, Ellen. *We Are Here: Memories of the Lithuanian Holocaust.* Lincoln: University of Nebraska Press, 2012.
Celan, Paul. Acceptance Speech, Bremen Prize for German Literature, 1958.
Čarževskienė, Irena. Interview. Vilnius: Lithuania Documentation Project, 1998, 2000–2001: USHMM: RG-50.473.015.
Chiger, Krystyna. *The Girl in the Green Sweater.* New York: St. Martin's Press, 2008.
Damasio, Antonio. "An Interview with Antonio R. Damasio." Interview by Conor Liston. *The Harvard Brain* 8 (2001): 2.
Delbo, Charlotte. *Days and Memory.* Translated by Rosette Lamont. Evanston, IL: Marlboro Press, 2001.
Dieckmann, Christoph, Vytautas Toleikis, and Rimantas Zizas. *Murders of Prisoners and War and of Civilian Population in Lithuania.* Vilnius: International Commission for the Evaluation of the Crimes of the Nazi and Soviet Occupation Regimes in Lithuania, 2005.
Dieckmann, Christoph, and Saulius Sužiedėlis. *The Persecution and Mass Murder of Lithuanian Jews during Summer and Fall of 1941.* Vilnius: International

Commission for the Evaluation of the Crimes of the Nazi and Soviet Occupation Regimes in Lithuania, 2006.

Donskis, Leonidas, and Zygmunt Bauman. *Moral Blindness*. Cambridge, UK: Polity Press, 2013.

Edwards, Scott P. "The Amygdala: The Body's Alarm Circuit." *Brain Work: The Neuroscience Newsletter* 15, no. 3 (2005).

Eidintas, Alfonsas. *Jews, Lithuanians, and the Holocaust*. Vilnius: Versus Aureus, 2003.

Eilati, Shalom. *Crossing the River*. Tuscaloosa: University of Alabama Press, 2008.

———. *Crossing the River*. Prepublication manuscript.

Elkes, Joel. *Dr. Elkhanan Elkes of the Kovno Ghetto: A Son's Memoir*. Brewster, MA: Paraclete Press, 1999.

Felman, Shoshana, and Dori Laub. *Testimony: Crisis of Witnessing in Literature, Psychoanalysis, and History*. New York: Routledge, 1992.

Ganor, Solly. *Light One Candle: A Survivor's Tale from Lithuania to Jerusalem*. New York: Kodansha America, 1995.

Garfunkel, Leib. *The Destruction of the European Jews*. Jerusalem: Yad Vashem, 1963.

Gelpernas, Dimitri, and Meir Yelin. *Partisans of Kovno Ghetto*. Translated by Robin O'Neil, 1996.

Gilligan, James. *Violence: Reflections on a National Epidemic*. New York: Vintage Books, 1997.

Ginaitė-Rubinson, Sara. *Resistance and Survival: The Jewish Community in Kaunas 1941–1945*. Oakville, Ontario: Mosaic Press, 2005.

Grand, Sue. *The Reproduction of Evil: A Clinical & Cultural Perspective*. Hillsdale, NJ: The Analytic Press, 2002.

Greenspan, Henry. *On Listening to Holocaust Survivors: Recounting and Life History*. Westport, CT: Praeger Press, 1998.

Gruber, Samuel, and Phyllis Myer. *The Survey of Historical Jewish Monuments in Poland: A Report of the U.S. Commission of Preservation of America's Heritage Abroad*.

Hallie, Phillip. *Lest Innocent Blood Be Shed*. New York: Harper and Row, 1979.

Halter, Marek. *Stories of Deliverance*. Chicago: Open Court, 1998.

Hamman. S. B., L. R. Squire, and D. S. Schacter. "Perceptual Threshold and Priming in Amnesia." *Neuropsychology* 9 (1995): 3–15.

Hands Bringing Life and Bread: Volume 1. Vilnius: The Vilna Gaon Jewish State Museum, 1997.

Hartmann, Ernest. *The Nature and Functions of Dreaming*. Oxford: Oxford University Press, 2011.

Hartman, Geoffrey H. *The Longest Shadow: In the Aftermath of the Holocaust*. Bloomington: Indiana University Press, 1996.

Herman, Judith. *Trauma and Recovery*. New York: Basic Books, 1992.
Hilliard, Robert L. *Surviving the Americans: The Continued Struggle for the Jews after Liberation*. New York: Seven Stories Press, 1996.
Hoffman, Eva. *Shtetl*. New York: Houghton Mifflin, 1997.
Holocaust and Genocide Studies 13, no. 1 (1999). Oxford: Oxford University Press and the U.S. H. M. M.
Homefront: Stories of America at War, a student-created documentary. Produced by Rick Rockwell. American University School of Communications, 2007.
Inčiūrienė, Yocheved. Interview by Myra Sklarew. Kaunas, Lithuania, 1996.
Jacobson, Dan. "Lithuanian Pastoral." *Commentary* 104, no. 4 (October 1997): 34–38.
Jasiūnas, Rimgaudas. Interview. Vilnius: Lithuania Documentation Project, 1998, 2000–2001: USHMM: RG-50.473.017.
Juknaitė, Vanda. *My Voice Betrays Me*. Boulder, CO: East European Monographs, 2007.
Kandel, Eric. *In Search of Memory; The Emergence of a New Science of Mind*. New York: W. W. Norton, 2006.
Katz, Dovid. "A New Book about the Cultural Life in the Vilna Ghetto." Review of *Spiritual Resistance in the Vilna Ghetto*, by Rachel Kostanian. *The Yiddish Forward*, August 16, 2002 (Translated by Miriam Dashkin Beckerman, Canada).
Kenez, Peter. *Varieties of Fear: Growing Up Jewish Under Nazism and Communism*. Bloomington, IN: iUniverse, 2001.
Kestenberg, Judith, and Charlotte Kahn, eds. *Children Surviving Persecution: An International Study of Trauma and Healing*. Westport, CT: Praeger, 1998.
Kestenberg, Judith, and Ira Brenner. *The Last Witness—The Child Survivor of the Holocaust*. American Psychiatric Publishing, 1966.
Klein Halevi, Yossi. "Murderers, She Wrote." *The Jerusalem Report*, November 14, 1996.
Kostanian, Rachel, Ralph Levie, Henri Minczeles, Ives Plasseraud, Liudas Truska, Hans de Vries, and Emanuelis, Zingeris, eds. *Atminties Dienos: The Days of Memory*. International Conference: Commemoration of the 50th Anniversary of the Liquidation of the Vilnius Ghetto. Vilnius: Baltos Lankos, 1993.
Kovner, Abba. *A Canopy in the Desert: Selected Poems*. Pittsburgh: University of Pittsburgh Press, 1973.
Kraft, Robert. *Memory Perceived: Recalling the Holocaust*. Westport, CT: Praeger, 2002.
Kunitz, Stanley. *Next to Last Things: New Poems and Essays*. New York: Atlantic Monthly Press, 1985.

Kuodytė, Dalia, and Rimantas Stankevičius. *Whoever Saves One Life . . . The Efforts to Save Jews in Lithuania between 1941 and 1944*. Vilnius: Genocide and Resistance Research Centre, 2002.
LaCapra, Dominick. *Writing History, Writing Trauma*. Baltimore: Johns Hopkins University Press, 2013.
Lang, Berel. *The Future of the Holocaust: Between History and Memory*. Ithaca: Cornell University Press, 1999.
Langer, Lawrence L. *Holocaust Testimonies: The Ruins of Memory*. New Haven: Yale University Press, 1991.
———. *Admitting the Holocaust*. Oxford: Oxford University Press, 1995.
Langosch, Rachel. "Lithuania: A Place to Remember; A Place to Forget." Student paper, Bard College, 2002.
———. Interview with Solly Ganor. 2002.
Laub, Dori, and Nanette C. Auerhahn, eds. "Knowing and Not Knowing the Holocaust." *Psychoanalytic Inquiry* 5, No. 1 (1985).
LeDoux, Joseph. *The Emotional Brain: The Mysterious Underpinnings of Emotional Life*. New York: Simon and Schuster, 1996.
———. "Parallel Memories: Putting Emotions Back into the Brain: A Talk with Joseph LeDoux." *Edge*, February 17, 1997. https://www.edge.org/conversation/joseph_ledoux-parallel-memories-putting-emotions-back-into-the-brain.
Levi, Primo. *The Drowned and the Saved*. New York: Summit Books, 1988.
Levin, Dov. *Fighting Back: Lithuanian Jewry's Armed Resistance to the Nazis, 1941–1945*. New York: Holmes and Meier, 1997.
Levinson, Joseph, ed. *The Shoah (Holocaust) in Lithuania*. Vilnius: The Vilna Gaon Jewish State Museum, 2006.
Lowenthal, David. *The Past is a Foreign Country*. Cambridge: Cambridge University Press, 1985.
Lithuanian Mythological Tales. Vilnius: Vaga, 2002.
Mackus, Algimantas. *Jurek*. Translated by Zita Sodeika. https://allpoetry.com/poem/8612045-Jurek-by-Algimantas-Mackus.
Mandelstam, Osep. *Selected Poems*. Translated by Clarence Brown and W. S. Merwin. New York: Atheneum, 1974.
Manea, Norman. *The Hooligan's Return: A Memoir*. New York: Farrar, Straus and Giroux, 2003.
Margalit, Avishai. *The Ethics of Memory*. Cambridge: Harvard University Press, 2002.
Miknevičienė, Elena. Unpublished manuscript, 1994.
Mintz, Alan. *Hurban*. New York: Syracuse University Press, 1996.
Mishell, William W. *Kaddish for Kovno: Life and Death in a Lithuanian Ghetto 1941–1945*. Chicago: Chicago Review Press, 1988.

"News & Views." *Nature* 381 (June 1996): 471–72.

Nayman, Shira. *Awake in the Dark*. New York: Simon and Schuster, 2006.

Niewyk, Donald L, ed. *Fresh Wounds: Early Narratives of Holocaust Survival* (David Boder Interviews). Chapel Hill: University of North Caroline Press, 1998.

Oliner, Samuel P., and Pearl M. Oliner. *The Altruistic Personality: Rescuers of Jews in Nazi Europe*. New York: The Free Press, 1988.

Oshry, Rabbi Ephraim. *The Annihilation of Lithuanian Jewry*. New York: Judaica Press, 1995.

———. *Responsa from the Holocaust*. New York: Judaica Press 1989.

Pagis, Dan. *The Selected Poetry of Dan Pagis*. Berkeley: University of California Press, 1996.

Paldiel, Mordecai. *Sheltering the Jews: Stories of Holocaust Rescuers*. Minneapolis: Fortress Press, 1996.

Pally, Regina. *The Mind-Brain Relationship*. Abingdon: Routledge, 2000.

Parens, Henri. *Renewal of Life: Healing from the Holocaust*. Rockville, MD: Schreiber, 2004.

Pliny the Younger. *The Epistles of Pliny the Younger*. Edinburgh: A. Donaldson and J. Reis, 1762.

Puišytė, Rūta. "Holocaust in Jurbarkas: The Mass Extermination of Jews of Jurbarkas in the Provinces of Lithuania during the German Nazi Occupation." BA thesis, Vilnius University, 1997, www.shtetlinks.jewishgen.org/yurburg/bathesis.html.

Radnoti, Miklos. *Clouded Sky*. New York: Sheep Meadow Press, 2003.

Ramachandran, V. S., and Sandra Blakeslee. *Phantoms in the Brain*. New York: William Morrow, 1998.

Raouf, Masoud, dir. *The Tree That Remembers*. 2002; Chicago: Olive Films, 2007. DVD.

Reber, P. J., and L. R. Squire. "Parallel Brain Systems for Learning with and without Awareness." *Learning and Memory* 1 (1994): 1–13.

Restak, Richard. "Rapid Response." Review of *The Emotional Brain: The Mysterious Underpinnings of Emotional Life*, by Joseph LeDoux. *New York Times Book Review*, Dec. 1, 1996. https://www.nytimes.com/1996/12/01/books/rapid-response.html.

Rilke, Rainer Maria. *The Poetry of Rainer Maris Rilke*. Translated by M. D. Herter Norton. New York: W. W. Norton, 1962.

Rosen, Alan. *The Wonder of Their Voices: The 1946 Holocaust Interviews of David Boder*. Oxford: Oxford University Press, 2010.

Rothberg, Michael. *Traumatic Realism: The Demands of Holocaust Representation*. Minneapolis: University of Minnesota Press, 2000.

Rothschild, Babette. *The Body Remembers: The Psychophysiology of Trauma and Trauma Treatment*. New York: W. W. Norton, 2000.

Rudashevski, Yitskhok. *The Diary of the Vilna Ghetto: June 1941-April 1943*. Israel: Ghetto Fighters' House, 1979.
Rurup, Reinhard, ed. *Topography of Terror*. Berlin: Verlag Wilmuth Arenhovel, 1989.
Sakowicz, Kazimierz. *Ponary Diary: 1941–1943: A Bystander's Account of a Mass Murder*. New Haven: Yale University Press, 2005.
Saunoris, Jean. Letter to Yad Vashem. Montreal. December 24, 1993.
Schafft, G. E., and William H. Kincade. "Holes in Their Histories: Public History and Public Policy." *International Studies Notes* 18, no. 2 (Spring 1983): 6–14.
Schalkowsky, Sam. *The Clandestine History of the Kovno Ghetto Police*. Bloomington: Indiana University Press, 2014.
Schore, Allan N. *Affect Regulation and the Origin of the Self: The Neurobiology of Emotional Development*. Hillsdale, NJ: Lawrence Erlbaum Associates, 1994.
Schwartz, Rosaline, and Susan Melamid. *A Guide to Yivo's Landmanshaftn Archives: From Alexandrovsk to Zyrardow*. New York: YIVO Insititute for Jewish Research, 1986.
Šilkinaitė, Vera. Interview by Saulius Beržinis. Translated by Anna Zlotak. Arranged by Myra Sklarew. Vilnius: Lithuania Documentation Project, 1998, 2000–2001: USHMM: RG-50.473.003.
Squire. L. R. "Memory and Forgetting: Long-term and Gradual Changes in Memory Storage." In *Selectionism and the Brain, Vol. 37 (International Review of Neurobiology)*, edited by O. Sporns and G. Tononi, 243–70. New York: Academic Press, 1994.
Squire, L. R., and B. J. Knowlton. "The Organization of Memory." In *The Mind, the Brain, and Complex Adaptive Systems*, edited by H. J. Morowitz and J. L. Singer, 63–98. Santa Fe Institute Series (Book 22). Abingdon: Routledge, 1995.
———. "Memory, Hippocampus, and Brain Systems." In *The Cognitive Neuroscience*, edited by M. Gazzaniga, 825–37. Cambridge: MIT Press, 1994.
Sruoginis, Laima. *Lithuania: In Her Own Words*. Vilnius: Tyto Alba, 1997.
Steinlauf, Michael, *Bondage to the Dead: Poland the Memory of the Holocaust*. Syracuse: Syracuse University Press, 1997.
Sten, Ephraim F. *1111 Days in My Life Plus Four*. Takoma Park: Dryad Press, 2006.
Stevens, C. F. "Strengths and Weaknesses in Memory." *Nature*, 381, no. 6582 (June 6, 1996): 471–72.
"Sugihara House: Between the Past and the Present." Museum Document, Sugihara House, Kaunas, Lithuania.
Šukys, Julija. *And I Burned with Shame: The Testimony of Ona Simaite, Righteous Among the Nations, A Letter to Isaac Nachman Steinberg (Search and Research, Band 10)*. Göttingen: Wallstein Verlag GmbH, 2008.

Suleiman, Susan Rubin. *Crises of Memory and the Second World War*. Cambridge: Harvard University Press, 2006.

Sužiedėlis, Saulius. "The Burden of 1941," *Lituanus* 47, no. 4 (Winter 2001).

———. *Holocaust in Lithuania in the Focus of Modern History, Education and Justice: The Mass Persecution and Murder of Jews: The Summer and Fall of 1941*. Paper presented at the International Conference on Holocaust Research and Education, Vilnius, Lithuania, September 2002.

Trouillot, Michel-Rolph. *Silencing the Past: Power and the Production of History*. Boston: Beacon Press, 1995.

Truitt, Anne. *Turn: The Journal of an Artist*. New York: Penguin Press, 1987.

Trunk, Isaiah. *Judenrat, The Jewish Councils in Eastern Europe Under Nazi Occupation*. New York: Stein and Day, 1977.

Truska, Liudas. *The Upsurge of Antisemitism in Lithuania in the Years of the Soviet Occupation (1940–1941)*. Vilnius: 2001.

———, and Vygantas Vareikis. *The Preconditions for the Holocaust: Anti-Semitism in Lithuania*. Vilnius: The International Commission for the Evaluation of the Crimes of the Nazi and Soviet Occupation Regimes in Lithuania, 2004.

Van der Kolk, Bessel, Alexander C. McFarlane, and Lars Weisaeth. *Traumatic Stress*. New York: The Guilford Press, 1996.

Volkan, Vamik. *Killing in the Name of Identity*. Virginia: Pitchstone, 2006.

Wiesel, Elie. *The Gates of the Forest*. New York: Schocken, 1995.

Wolpe, David E. *Ich un Main Welt (I and My World)*. Johannesburg-Jerusalem: 1997.

———. *Ich un Main Welt (I and My World)*. Manuscript. Translated by Miriam Beckerman.

Young, James E. *Writing and Rewriting the Holocaust: Narrative and the Consequences of Interpretation*. Bloomington: Indiana University Press, 1988.

———. *The Texture of Memory: Holocaust Memorials and Meaning*. New Haven: Yale University Press, 1993.

Zabludoff, Olga, and Lily Poritz Miller, eds. *A Thousand Threads: A Story Told through Yiddish Letters*. Translated by Miriam Beckerman. Washington, DC: Remembrance Books, 2005.

———. *I Forget Thee . . . The Destruction of the Shtetl Burtimantz*. Washington, DC: Remembrance Books, 1998.

Zola-Morgan, S., L. R. Squire, and S. J. Ramus. "Severity of Memory Impairment in Monkeys as a Function of Locus and Extent of Damage within the Medial Temporal Lobe Memory System." *Hippocampus* 4 (1994): 482–95.

index

Adomavičius, Jonas, 139, 141–42
Adorno, Theodor, 13
Agnon, S. Y., 13
Akedah (Genesis), 46
Aleksotas, 108
Alter, Robert, 12
Alytus, 52, 83
Ältestenrat, xiv, 12, 59, 75, 179
Amery, Jean, 13, 19–20
Amichai, Yehuda, xiv, 13
Appelfeld, Aharon, 20
Ariogala, 34, 71
Auschwitz Concentration Camp, 11, 13, 19, 67, 84, 181
Austrian Holocaust Memorial Service. *See* Gedenkdienst

Babtai, 34, 71
Bad Worishölen, 70
Baisigola, 34
Balandienė, Aleksandra (Ola), xiv, 100–104
Balandienė, Balandis, 101
Baltimore, Maryland (USA), 53–54
Banditen (Bandits), 37
Bar-On, Daniel, 84
Baublys, Dr. Petras, 134–36, 152, 193n3 (chap. VIII)

Baublys, Rostis, 136
BBC, 155
Beckett, Samuel, 13
Beržinis, Povilas, 157
Beržinis, Saulius, xiv, 155–59, 175
Beržinis, Viktoras, 156
Bet Guvrin, 31–32
Birger, Zev, 118, 191
Birštonas, 155
Borges, Jorge Luis, 9, 124–25
Braun, Moshe, 60
Breznitz, Shlomo, 17
Bunke, Jacob, xiv, 76
Butkutė, Efinija, 135
Butrimantz. *See* Butrimonys
Butrimonys, 52, 175, 177–78

Care (film), 159
Čarževskienė, Irena, 86–87, 190n2 (chap. V)
Celan, Paul, 13, 21
Center for Tolerance, 194n1 (chap. IX)
Chagall, Marc, 61
Charles E. Smith Jewish Day School, 108
Chiger, Krystyna, 37–38
Children's Aktion. *See* Kinder Aktion

Chmielnicki, 49
Čiurlionis, Mikalojus Konstantinas, 164
Culture Federation of South Africa, 172

Dachau Concentration Camp, ix, 14, 16, 31, 57, 59, 62, 69–71, 73–74, 78, 80, 98, 106, 118, 131, 134, 172, 179, 180
Damasio, Antonio R., 123, 124
Dante, 23, 47–48, 129
Davidavičius, Simonas, x, xiv, 143, 170–71
Delbo, Charlotte, 19
Dotnuva, 25, 32, 34, 71, 84, 96, 99–101, 103–106
Druskininkai, 161

Efros, Esther, 163
Eilati, Shalom, xiv, 119–23, 130, 178–79, 190n4 (chap. IV), 191n11 (chap. VII), 191n13 (chap. VII)
Einsatzgruppen, 16, 27–28
Elijošaitis, Bronius, xiv, 137–39
Eliošaičiai, Ona, 138
Eliošaičiai, Pranas, 138
Elkes, Elchanan, xiv, 12, 59, 75, 179
Elkes, Joel, xiv, 59
End of the Road (film), 159

Farewell, Jerusalem of Lithuania (film), 156, 159
Finland, Embassy, 155
Fischer, Obershaffer, 34–35
Forest Brothers, 37
Forest Partisans, 37

Frank, Anne, 50, 167
French Resistance, 187n3
Freud, Sigmund, 123–24

Gan Eden (Garden of Eden), 16, 178
Ganor, Solly, xiv, 74, 112, 179–80
Gaon of Vilna. *See* Vilna Gaon
Garbaravičius, Ramūnas, 170
Garfunkel, Leib, 190n4 (chap. IV)
Gautien, 58
Gedenkdienst (Austrian Holocaust Memorial Service), 7–8, 49, 167
Gehinom (Hell), 16
Gelpernas, Dimitri, xiv, 88
Gestapo, 108, 134–36, 138
Gilboa, Amir, 12
Ginaitė-Rubinson, Sara, 171
Girtigola, 34, 71
Glatstein, Jacob, 109
Great Aktion, 77, 80, 119–20
Gribauskaitė, Dalia, 193n12 (chap. VIII)
Grigaliūnaitė-Pažemeckienė, Apolonija, 135
Grodno, Belarus, 161

Hebrew, xi, 12, 37, 49, 52, 53, 65, 96, 103, 107, 148, 160, 163, 166, 173, 177
Hebrew Immigrant Aid Society (HIAS), 107
Hecht, Eta, xiv, 181
Herman, Edward, 71
Herman, Judith, 122–23
HIAS. *See* Hebrew Immigrant Aid Society
Hilliard, Robert, 71
Hitler, Adolf, 49, 60, 69

Humanist of the Year Award
  (Embassy of Finland and Rogatchi
  Foundation), 155

Inčiūra, Jurgis, 142–43
Inčiūrienė, Marytė. *See* Šimukėnaitė,
  Marytė
Inčiūrienė, Yocheved Cartok, xiv,
  17–18, 133, 137–43, 183, 190n1
  (chap. V), 193n10 (chap. VIII)
Independent Holocaust Archive of
  Lithuania, 155–56, 158–59
Inferno. See Dante
International Commission for the
  Evaluation of the Crimes of the
  Nazi and Soviet Occupation
  Regimes in Lithuania, 40
Iraq War, vii, 42, 109, 129–30

Jakūbėnas, Kazys, 139
Jasaitytė, Marcelė, 135
Jasiūnaitė, Genė [Genovaitė], 157
Jaspon, Yetta Helen, 32–34
Johannesburg, South Africa, 78, 172
Joint Distribution Committee, xiv,
  107
Josvainiai, 31, 32–34, 71, 104, 106
Judenrat (Jewish councils), 19
Jurbarkas, 156, 167

Kacerginski (family), 60
Kafka, Franz, 13
Kagan, Zundel, 103
Kaiserwald Concentration Camp,
  34–35
Kaišiadorys, 36
Kalmonovitch, Zelig Hirsh, 166–67
Kanovitch, Sergey, 159
Katz, Dovid, xiv, 165

Kaufman, Shirley, 29
Kaunas, x, 8, 9, 16, 52, 55, 59, 67,
  73, 74, 83, 85, 103, 106, 118,
  120, 136, 138, 139, 140, 141,
  143, 162, 168, 170, 171. *See also*
  Kovno
Kaunas Ghetto. *See* Kovno Ghetto
Kaunas Technological University, 171
Keidan, vii, 25, 34, 36, 55, 56, 59,
  63, 66, 69, 73, 81, 82, 96, 98,
  99, 144–53, 160, 184
Kėdainiai. *See* Keidan
Kėdainiai Cheder, 148
Kėdainiai Massacre Place Memorial,
  144–47
Kėdainiai Regional Museum, 81–82,
  144–53
Kempner, Vitka, xiv, 30
Kenez, Peter, 14
KGB, 151, 187n4
Khurban Museum (Vilnius), 165–66
Kiel, Germany, 16, 106
Kincade, William H., 18
Kinder Aktion, 67, 118, 120–21,
  181, 190n4 (chap IV)
Klaipėda, 60
Klein, George, 164
Knipovith, Rabbi, 157
Kopa, Film Studio, 155–59
Kopilevich, Regina, x, xiii, 96–99,
  101, 110, 159–64
Kosofsky, Rabbi, 67
Kostanian, Rachel, x, xiv, 164–67
Kovner, Abba, xiv, 28–31, 134
Kovno, 34. *See also* Kaunas
Kovno Ältestenrat. *See* Ältestenrat
Kovno (Kaunas) Ghetto, ix, xiv, 12,
  14, 16, 29, 31, 55, 56, 60, 66,
  67, 69, 75, 77, 78, 88–89,

208 INDEX

Kovno (Kaunas) Ghetto *(continued)* 95, 98, 106–107, 115–19, 130, 134–35, 138–40, 171, 172, 179, 181, 190n4 (chap IV), 191n4 (chap. V)
Kraft, Robert, 42
Krak, 34, 71, 103
Krakės. See *Krak*
Krost, Masha, 98
Kruk, Herman, 167
Kunitz, Stanley, 32, 104
Kurklietiene-Žemkalnienė, Dr. E., 135

Laisvės Alėja (Freedom Way), 55, 57, 60, 71, 73, 74, 78, 108, 118, 190n4 (chap. VII)
Landsbergis, Vytautas, 164, 193n12 (chap. VIII)
Langosch, Rachel, xiv, 101, 110–13
Latvia-Lithuania-Belarus Programme, 153
Lažai, 149
Le Chambon, France, 5–6, 137
LeDoux, Joseph, 123, 126–28
Levi, Primo, 19, 20
Levinsteinaitė, Sara, 102
Levitt, Leah, 163
Lidelange Concentration Camp (France), 134
Lietūkis Garage Massacre, ix, 17, 83–91
Lilienblum, Moshe-Leib, 99, 147
linking objects, 51
Lithuania, language(s), xi, 96, 110, 141, 160, 162–63, erasure, 38, 115–18, 135. See also *specific languages*
Lithuania, occupations, 5

Lithuania, population, 4–5
Lithuanian Activist Front (LAF), 37, 139, 177
Lithuanian Documentation Project, 125–26
Lithuanian Jewish Community Council, 171
Litvak Yiddish, 96, 103–104, 158, 159
Lodz, Poland, vii, 35–36
Lopaiko, Feiga Masha, 106
Lopaiko, Leah, 100, 102–103
Lopaiko, Rena, 100, 102
Lopaiko, Shimon, 100, 102
Lopšelis Children's Home, 134–37, 152
Lovely Faces of the Killers (film), 156, 159
Lozansky-Bogomolnaya, Riva, 175–78, 184
Lukošius, 149
Lunsky, Chaikl, 166
Luria, Alexander, 123
Luria, Shalom, 166
Lvov, Poland, 37, 130

Mackus, Algimantas, 39
MacLean, Paul, 126–27
Mahler, Gustav, 130
malina (hiding place), 49
Mandelstam, Osip, 182
Mankiškiai, 141–42
March of the Living (Molėtai), 152, 193n12 (chap. VIII)
Margolis, Rachel, 27
Marija, Marija (song), 104
Matiukas, Pranas, 187n4
Menkes, Sara, 27–29
Mfitzai Haskala (library), 166–67

Miknevičienė, Elena, xiv, 136
Milosz, Czeslaw, 153
Mintis, Publishing House, 156
Mishell, William, 88–89
Molėtai, 152
Molodovsky, Kadya, 13
Molotov-Ribbentrop Pact, 15
Molskis, Feliksas, 139
Mongirdas, Vladas, 139
Morgenstern, Tsherna, 27–29
Munch, Edvard, 68

Nabriskey (Doctor), 75, 79
National Drama Theatre, 157
Nayman, Shira, 52–53
Ninth American Army, 80
Ninth Fort, ix, 67, 74, 77, 80, 115, 119, 181, 190n4 (chap. IV)
NKVD, 18, 103
Noshpitz, Charlotte, xiv, 181–82, 184

Oberst, 89–90
occupation (Nazi), Lithuania, viii, 5, 15–16, 31, 39, 40, 55, 59, 84, 115, 121, 133–34, 141, 149, 167
occupation (Soviet), Lithuania, viii, xiii, 4–5, 15, 18, 26, 31, 39, 40, 55, 90, 133, 149, 155, 162, 167
Ochs, Sheila, 108
Olkinaitė, Matilda, 158
Olympics bombing (Atlanta 1996), 127
Open Society Foundation, 41
Oppenheim, Chaim, 66, 184
Oshry, Rabbi Ephraim, 48–49, 67
"Oyfn Pripetchik" (song), 109

Pagis, Dan, 12
Palanga, 71, 78, 119

Pally, Regina, 125
Paneriai Forest. *See* Ponar Forest
Paulauskienė, Zofija, 139
Perestroika, 162
Peskin, Harvey, 47
Petrified Time, The (film), 159
Platoon (film), 129
Pliny the Younger, 14–15
Plungė, 76–77
Pompeii, 9–10, 14–15
Ponar Forest, 17, 23–37
Ponevezh, 34, 71
Pribram, Karl, 184, 195n13 (chap. X)
Puišytė, Rūta, x, xiv, 167
Punia. *See* Punija
Punija, 52

Rabin, Yitzhak, 120
Radnoti, Miklos, 12, 16
Radviliada. *See* Radziwills
Radziwills, Dukes, 33, 153
Rashe Forest, 157
Rasein, 34, 71
Resnick, Abe, 162
Rilke, Rainer Maria, 77–78, 80
Rimgaudas, Jasiūnas, 87–88, 191n3 (chap. V)
Rivera, Diego, 76
Road to Treblinka, The (film), 156
Rogatchi Foundation, 155
Ronder, Yudel, xiv, 35–36, 98–99, 160
Rozewicz, Tadeusz, 50
Rothberg, Michael, 13
Ruseiniai, 34, 71
Russell, Paul, 79

Sachs, Nelly, 13
Sajūdis, 150, 162

Sakowicz, Kazimierz, 26–27
Saukotas, 142–43
Šaulių Sąjunga (Rifleman's Association), 26–27
Saunoris (family), 140–43
Saunoris, Edmund, 141
Saunoris, Jean, 143
Saunoris, Jonas, 18, 140–41
Schafft, G. E., 18, 188
Schalkowsky, Sam, xiv, 34, 116–17, 123, 131
Schama, Simon, 4
Seimas (parliament, Lithuania), 162
Selbstverteidgungstruppen (Self-Defense Groups), 37
Šėta, 147
Shadova, 34
Shadove Jewish Memorial fund, 159
Shaulists, 26, 37
Shavl, 71, 165
Shoah Foundation, 109, 131
Šiauliai, 34, 106, 138
Siberia (exile), viii, x, 18, 39, 85, 104–105, 133, 141, 144, 147, 149–51, 157
Silkinaitė, Vera, 85–86, 190n1 (chap. V)
Šimaitė, Ona, 134
Šimukėnaitė, Marytė, 139, 141–43
Slobodka, 55, 78–79. *See* Vilijampolė
Solc, Max, 88–89
Solms, Marc, 123–24
Sonderkommando, 18
Spielberg, Steven, Visual History Foundation, 171
St. Ottilien, 58, 70
Stafford, William, 6
Stalin, Joseph, 157

Steinlauf, Michael, 4
Sten, Ephraim, 12, 49–51, 173–74
Sten, Hagit, 173
Sten, Oded, 173
Stepaičiai, Jonas Adomavičius. *See* Adomavičius, Jonas
Stutthof Concentration Camp, 16, 57, 63, 67, 79, 80, 106, 131
Sugihara, Chiune, x, 164, 168–71
Sugihara Foundation, 170
Sugihara Museum (Kaunas), x, 143, 164, 168–71
Surviliškis, 149, 151
Sutzkever, Avrom/Avraham, 12, 167
Sužiedėlis, Saulius, xiv, 39–40
Syria, 42, 123

Tauragė, 138
Tautininkų sąjunga (National Party), 151
TDA (National Labor Guard), 37
Tel Aviv, Israel, 50, 179
Telz, 34
Tessin, Germany, 58, 62, 68, 73
Trocme, Magda, 6, 187n3
Trocme, Pastor, 5–6
Truitt, Anne, 187n1
Tyz, Hrye, 173

Ukmerge, 34
United Partisan Organization, 29–30
United States Holocaust Memorial Museum, 108, 116, 155, 162, 171
Utena, 157
Utian, 34, 71

Vallejo, Cesar, 45–46
Van der Kolk, Bessel, 123, 127, 130

Vandziogala (Vendzhigola), 34, 71
Varniai concentration camp, 138
Varzhan, 34
Veisaitė, Irena, 40–41
Venclova, Tomas, 152
Vietnam War, 47–48, 129
Vilijampolė, 55, 56, 57, 78–79, 134, 152, 171
Vilkomir, 34, 71
Vilna, city. *See* Vilnius
Vilna Gaon, 99, 147
Vilna Gaon Jewish Memorial, 7–8
Vilna Gaon Jewish State Museum, x, 7, 49, 134, 155, 164, 189, 193, 194
Vilna (Vilnius) Ghetto, 17, 27, 29, 134, 163, 165
Vilnius, 17, 27–29, 33, 34, 52, 71, 95–96, 99, 110, 156, 158, 163, 164, 166, 179–80
Vilnius University, x, 162, 167
Vilnius Yiddish Institute, 167
Vitonytė, Praneiška, 135, 136
Voice of America, 150
Volkan, Vamik D., 50–51
Volpe (family). *See* Wolpe

Waneustrasse, 67
Wehrmacht, 7
Weisenthal, Simon, Center, 177
Weissbindentragern (White Armbands), 37
When Yiddish Was Spoken Around Yanishek (film), 159
When Yiddish Was Spoken Around Yourbourk (film), 159
Wiesel, Elie, 14, 51, 108
Wolpe (family), xiv, 33, 66, 102–103
Wolpe (gravestone), 31–32

Wolpe, Abraham, 106
Wolpe, Ada Lipschitz, xiv–xv, 55, 58, 59, 61–62, 64–66, 68, 74–77, 81, 82, 190n1 (chap. IV)
Wolpe, Anne, ii, xiv
Wolpe, David E., 29–31, 70, 71, 98, 172, 184–85, 190n2 (chap. IV), 191–92n4 (chap VII)
Wolpe, Don, 109
Wolpe, Eliahu Akiba, 104, 106
Wolpe, Eliezer Semach, 34
Wolpe, Elisha, 106
Wolpe, Heshel, 106
Wolpe, Leiser, ix, xiv, 14, 55–82, 83, 98, 118–19, 190n2 (chap. IV), 191–92n4 (chap. V)
Wolpe, Luba Damarecki, 79
Wolpe, Jacob (Jankel), 16, 100, 106
Wolpe, Julius, 106–107
Wolpe Baras, Masha, 100, 105–10, 117, 131
Wolpe, Meyer Aaron, ii, xiv, 34
Wolpe, Pearl, 106
Wolpe, Sheine Solsky, 106

Yad Vashem, 36, 69, 120, 134, 136, 141, 143, 155, 192n11 (chap. VII)
Yaddo, 187n1
Yanova, 34, 71
Yashwen. *See* Josvainiai
Yiddish language, x, xi, 4, 37, 62–63, 65, 72, 96, 103, 104, 116, 159, 160, 163, 166, 167, 181, 190n4 (chap. IV). *See also* Litvak Yiddish
Yiddish place names, 34
Yiddish schools, 148

Yiddish songs, 109, 157
Yigdal, 12
Yosvine, 71
Yudel's Unwritten Diary (film), 156, 159

Zacherkhan (family), 60
Zarikhina, Mariya, 157
Žeimiai, 147

Zhirgunai, 73
Zingeris, Emanuel, xiv, 162
Žirgulis, Rimantas, xiv, 81, 97, 113, 144–53
Zloczow, Poland, 49–50
Zwartendijk, Jan, 168
Zurich, Switzerland, 55, 57, 59, 61, 64–65, 69, 73
Zuroff, Efraim, 177

www.ingramcontent.com/pod-product-compliance
Lightning Source LLC
Chambersburg PA
CBHW030650230426
43665CB00011B/1026